The Faithful Apologist comes from the biblically
of the careful Reformed theologian Scott Oliphint, and as such it provides
meticulous theological reflection on how persuasion takes place by and
through God's word and the measured use of classical rhetorical realities.
The result is a theologian's compelling *cri de coeur* to follow the graced
scriptural path to gospel persuasion—as commended by St. Paul—"Be
wise in the way you act toward outsiders; make the most of every opportunity. Let your conversation be always full of grace, seasoned with salt,
so that you may know how to answer everyone" (Col 4:5–6). This is a
foundational book, an indispensable prolegomenon to persuasion, and
will serve the church well, not only in personal evangelism but in the
preaching of the gospel to a lost world.

> R. KENT HUGHES, senior pastor emeritus,
> College Church, Wheaton, Illinois

Dr. Scott Oliphint is well-known as an academic theologian and apologist
who has devoted himself to matters of the intellect, but he has also been
a pastor who has devoted himself to people. In *The Faithful Apologist* he
helps us understand the importance of both devotions—not only in terms
of the way we think, or even the people we address, but in terms of who
we—the apologists—are. Some readers will be intrigued or even surprised
at first sight by his skilful (but very welcome!) borrowing from Aristotle's
insistence on the triad of *logos*, *ethos*, and *pathos* in all good communication. But in doing so, Oliphint touches on principles embedded in the
biblical doctrine of the image of God and that are constantly exhibited
and illustrated in Scripture but often overlooked by Christians.

The Faithful Apologist carries an important message for us all, remi-
niscent of the opening words of E. M. Bounds's famous book on prayer
("The church is looking for better methods, God is looking for better
men"). Scott Oliphint reminds us that while the church is looking for
better apologetics, God himself is looking for *better apologists*.

> DR. SINCLAIR B. FERGUSON, Ligonier teaching
> fellow and Chancellor's Professor of Systematic
> Theology, Reformed Theological Seminary

Christian apologetics has come a long way since being gagged by the "crisis theology" of Karl Barth. The defense of the faith is once more a legitimate endeavor. Yet there is a view abroad that all we need to do is amass evidence until rational people yield and admit the Christian faith is true. Unfortunately, reasonable people are becoming rare. Now is the time for persuasion. Very little work has been done on the biblical basis for persuasion. Dr. Oliphint's contribution is invaluable. His working definition is "the discerning and initiating of a *connection* between two or more persons." If that sounds abstract, Oliphint points us to the entire Bible, and especially to Jesus Christ, whose mission was "a design of divine persuasion." The reason? God's great love, which issues in his "condescension." In keeping with that, Oliphint has remarkable pages on certain passages, such as Romans 1, Acts 17, and 1 Peter 3, worth the price of the book. This book should be read and enjoyed by all Christians wanting to recover the art of persuasion.

WILLIAM EDGAR, professor of apologetics, Westminster
Theological Seminary, Philadelphia, Pennsylvania

The
FAITHFUL
Apologist

The
FAITHFUL
Apologist

RETHINKING *THE* ROLE *OF* PERSUASION *IN* APOLOGETICS

K. SCOTT OLIPHINT

ZONDERVAN ACADEMIC

ZONDERVAN ACADEMIC

The Faithful Apologist
Copyright © 2022 by K. Scott Oliphint

Requests for information should be addressed to:
Zondervan, *3900 Sparks Dr. SE, Grand Rapids, Michigan 49546*

Zondervan titles may be purchased in bulk for educational, business, fundraising, or sales promotional use. For information, please email SpecialMarkets@Zondervan.com.

978-0-310-14025-2 (audio)

Library of Congress Cataloging-in-Publication Data

Names: Oliphint, K. Scott, 1955- author.
Title: The faithful apologist : rethinking the role of persuasion in apologetics / K. Scott Oliphint.
Description: Grand Rapids : Zondervan, 2022.
Identifiers: LCCN 2021035007 (print) | LCCN 2021035008 (ebook) | ISBN 9780310590101 (paperback) | ISBN 9780310590125 (ebook)
Subjects: LCSH: Apologetics. | Influence (Psychology)--Religious aspects--Christianity. | Bible--Evidences, authority, etc.
Classification: LCC BT1103 .O454 2022 (print) | LCC BT1103 (ebook) | DDC 239--dc23/eng/20211021
LC record available at https://lccn.loc.gov/2021035007
LC ebook record available at https://lccn.loc.gov/2021035008

Cover design: LUCAS Art & Design
Cover photo: © inbj / Masterfile
Interior design: Kait Lamphere

Printed in the United States of America

22 23 24 25 26 27 28 29 30 31 32 /TRM/ 15 14 13 12 11 10 9 8 7 6 5 4 3 2 1

CONTENTS

INTRODUCTION

Almost immediately after my conversion to Christ, I was eager to tell people what had happened to me so they might have the same experience. I became a volunteer leader in an evangelistic ministry, and it was not long before I had the opportunity to communicate to others the joy and reality of my own conversion. I wanted both to commend and to defend the Christian faith. One occasion from those early days sticks out in my memory—a conversation with a man who had become a good friend.

I remember my almost desperate desire that this man be converted. I wanted to tell him all I had learned and to defend its truth if needed. I sat down with him one day and began to explain the gospel to him. I talked about God as our Creator. I explained how sin had entered our world through Adam. I gave him examples of sin's effects in almost every aspect of the world today.

Then I recounted to him the story of Christmas and told him the good news of the cross of Christ, his resurrection, and ascension. I then told him that, like the Philippian jailer, all that was required on our part was to believe in Christ and we would be saved. I flooded him with as much information as I could muster.

As a young and inexperienced Christian, I was greatly encouraged that throughout the discussion, he was nodding in agreement with everything I said. I was ready to defend it all, but he had no real objections. It all seemed to be so seamless and easy. I don't recall that he had even a single question for me.

When I had said everything I knew to say, I asked him if he was ready to make a commitment and to believe in Christ. He answered with a single word: "No."

I was stunned. I asked him, given what I had said, why he wasn't ready to make a commitment. His response still rings in my ears: "Nothing you have said indicates that I *need* this. I can't see the need for a commitment." His response devastated me, though I tried not to show it.

This encounter has been embedded in my memory for a few decades now. One reason for that, surely, is that it was one of my first experiences attempting to convince someone of something I was so passionately committed to. I saw myself in those nascent days as a true apologist for Christianity.

Another reason it has stuck with me is that, upon later reflection, it became clear to me that my only goal in that conversation was to impart as much information as I could. There is nothing intrinsically wrong with telling people the truth of the gospel, but through that entire conversation, I failed to connect what I was telling him to his own life, his own beliefs, his own needs, his own experiences. As a matter of fact, I don't think I was concerned about those aspects of his life at all. I don't remember asking him any questions about his own life.

My only concern was to tell the truth, and I assumed that was all I needed to bring him to a commitment. But I was wrong. In my conversation with him about the gospel, I should have focused not only on the truth of the message I wanted to defend, as glorious as that truth is, but also on how I might connect that glorious message with his experiences, bridging the gap between his own life and his need for the gospel. I should have focused on commending those gospel truths to him *persuasively*.

As we think together in the coming pages about apologetics and persuasion, we can define persuasion simply as our attempts to discern and initiate a connection between two or more people in order to defend and commend the gospel to them. Apologetics is concerned with defending the faith once and for all given to the saints (Jude 3). Persuasion is, at root, concerned with connecting that defense to those who might otherwise oppose it. By attempting to connect with them, a bridge is built between us and them so that our defense of the gospel and its truth can cross over from us to them.

Our subject in the coming pages is as exciting as it is elusive. It comes to us under two primary topics: apologetics and persuasion. With both of these, we will focus on the relationship of Christianity to its opponents and detractors. As we consider these two topics, we want to think about how the Word of God can be communicated by us in order to defend the Christian faith in a persuasive manner.

It might be that many will think of these two as opposites. Persuasion seeks and finds *connections* between two or more disparate viewpoints. Apologetics, on the other hand, tends to focus on *confrontation* as it seeks to meet objections against Christianity. We hope to make the case that these two are at their biblical and theological best when they merge together. We will also see that even as Christian apologetics seeks for *connections* between Christianity and those who would oppose it, so also can persuasion engage in *confrontation* between opposing views. The two topics, then, far from being mutually exclusive, sharpen each other as iron sharpens iron.

As a matter of fact, as we will see, these two topics substantially and significantly overlap, or at least they should. As we consider some of the primary aspects of them both, we will be focused on and interested in their *biblical and theological context*. That context needs to be set firmly in place in our minds and hearts, since it is foundational in order for apologetics and persuasion to successfully engage any other context— cultural or otherwise.

The proper context for persuasion and for apologetics is, in the first place, *Scripture*. Perhaps this sounds obvious; if so, very good. Too often, however, both topics can give the impression that they are each simply a matter of a proper *method* or *technique*.[1] If we can master a set of "theistic proofs," we might think, then our task in apologetics is mostly done. All that we need to do, no matter the situation, is to highlight the need for a "First Cause," or the rationality of a "Necessary Existence," and we have done our best and accomplished our goal to defend the faith.

Or perhaps we think that persuasion is nothing more than a sophisticated advertising campaign. We use a certain technique to create a need, and then "sell" our remedy to the need we have created. In other words, we create the need, then meet the need with our "product." Persuasion accomplished.

This kind of thinking about apologetics and persuasion is both subtle and dangerous. It is subtle for at least two reasons: First, there is an element of truth in the examples given above that can, when *properly* understood, provide help for us in our attempts to persuade people of the truth of the Christian faith and to defend that faith against objections and attacks. It certainly is the case that God is the first cause of all that exists (except Himself) and that He necessarily exists. But to think that is the central focus of Christian apologetics is to unduly short-circuit its richness and depth. We'll discuss this more later on.

Second, one of the primary allures of technique, which pervades our culture and society, is that, once learned, persuasion is easily accomplished. So, instead of diving below the superficial, we can begin to think that we can "bottle" a certain method of persuasion and then "pour it out" on anyone and everyone in exactly the same way. We are tempted to want a quick and easy fix for any and all objections that might come our way. We might resist complexity and patience, wanting instead a kind of "four spiritual laws" of persuasion or a "twelve-step program" of apologetics.

But apologetics and persuasion cannot be reduced to simple formulas or methods or techniques. Because both of them have to do, in the first place, with the Christian faith and its application to *people*, they are both

---

1. For one of the best and most accessible assessments of Christian persuasion and the problem of *technique*, see Os Guinness, *Fool's Talk: Recovering the Art of Christian Persuasion* (Downers Grove, IL: InterVarsity Press, 2015).

deeply and magnificently rooted in the truth of God and His revelation. That is to say, both apologetics and persuasion are, from top to bottom, *biblical and theological*. They have their initial *animus*, their *raison d'être*, their proper focus, in the rich and vibrant soil of God's Word.

Because of the central and crucial importance of Scripture in our apologetics and in persuasion, this book will provide some of the crucial biblical and theological truths that should inform our persuasive defense of Christianity. In that way, this book should be seen as a Bible study on persuasive apologetics. It is a biblical and theological introduction to a persuasive apologetic.

With that in view, the first three chapters will set out the biblical and theological foundations of our topic. In the second section, chapters 4 through 6, we will consider the art of persuasion as it is given and demonstrated to us in Holy Scripture. Because of our focus, it would be useful for you to have a Bible nearby throughout our discussion. I hope to explain some of the main contours of persuasion and apologetics as they relate to key aspects of biblical truth.

In the pages to come, you'll see there is a natural and automatic connection (biblically speaking) between the discipline of apologetics and the art of persuasion. This connection has not been prominent in much of the literature on apologetics. Typically, apologetics has been linked to the sometimes difficult and abstract thinking of philosophy, like two sides of a coin. Because of this, the goal that apologetics has often set for itself has been centered around the notion of demonstrative, philosophical "proofs."

Of course, there is nothing intrinsically wrong with a Christian interaction with, and even co-opting of, philosophical ideas and concepts. The history of theology is evidence of a faithful use of philosophy. And oftentimes, perhaps most times, the challenge that has been lodged against Christianity includes the demand to "prove" that God exists. That challenge, too, needs a response.

But apologetics is not, in the first place, a philosophical discipline. It was never meant to be reserved solely for academics and intellectuals who enjoy the thrill of debate. Apologetics is meant for the people of God (see 1 Pet 3:15). It is meant to express hope amid a hopeless and suffering world. If philosophical objections come against Christianity, as they often have, then it might be useful to try to answer them according to similar philosophical vocabulary. But that is just one aspect of the discipline of apologetics, not its core. Its core consists of biblical reasons for the hope that is ours in Christ.

We should not think, however, that apologetics has nothing to do with method or with philosophical ideas. Neither should we think that the demand for "proofs" rules out the possibility of persuasion. Instead, we should see all of these various notions—apologetics, proofs, philosophy, persuasion, and more besides—as in need (as is everything) of substantial and foundational biblical and theological roots.

With those roots firmly established, each notion, and all of them together, can grow in the proper soil and produce much fruit along the way. Without those rich roots, apologetics, proofs, philosophical ideas, and persuasion are sure to wither and die; they will be nothing more than lifeless weeds on a dry and parched ground.

Though our particular focus in this book will be a biblical study of the central aspects of apologetics and persuasion, we will need to broach the subject of philosophical proofs as well. Even as we do, the ultimate goal throughout our study will be that God would be honored and glorified in our thinking about these things, and in their doing. If that goal is accomplished in these pages, and in our lives, then, from the perspective of Scripture, we will have succeeded.

As we will see, "success" in apologetics and in persuasion, so far as it depends on us, can only be measured by our faithful thinking and living. It cannot, and must not, be measured by responses that we might receive as we attempt to defend and persuade people concerning the Christian faith.

In our defense, and in our persuasion, we must recognize that the triune *God*, and He alone, is the only one able to draw people to Himself. Our defense and our persuasion are done as means to His sovereign ends.

Introduction

But it is He, and He alone, who ultimately defends His glory, and who *actually* has the power to defend and to persuade. As we think biblically and theologically about apologetics and persuasion, these must be our starting points: God is the Divine Persuader, and God is the Divine Apologist.

In part 1, our study of Scripture will highlight those two crucial truths. We will then need to set firmly in place the foundation of the Word of God as our "weapon" in the battle with unbelief. Scripture reminds us that God's Word is like a sword, not only piercing our own hearts, but piercing through hard, unbelieving hearts in our spiritual battle (Heb 4:12; cf. Eph 6:17).

In part 2, we will look at Scripture from the perspective of three specific aspects of persuasion. Those three aspects focus on the *person* who is attempting to persuade, the *persons* to whom we speak, and the *message* we are attempting to convey. We will see how those aspects easily merge with our defense of Christianity. In those discussions, we will see how we can be properly commissioned into His service, as we seek to be, under Him, defenders of and persuaders toward the majestic truth of that great good news of the gospel, without which no one will see the Lord (Heb 12:14).

As we work through Scripture in order to highlight the relationship of apologetics and persuasion, each and every point made must be shrouded in and filtered by the central truth that God Himself is the Faithful Apologist and Persuader. That truth is both liberating and motivating. It is liberating because it reminds us that the actual work of changing human hearts belongs to Him alone. No amount of human ingenuity or attractive presentations will change a heart of stone to a heart of flesh. Our burden is not to try to "sell" the gospel to someone. Instead, our concern is to commend His truth in a wise way, a way that would connect that truth to our audience.

That God is our Faithful Apologist is motivating because the Lord, who alone is able to draw us to Himself (John 6:44), has given to us the means He uses to persuade others. It is our communication of His truth that He employs as the key to unlock hard hearts so they open up to the gospel. He has given us that key, and He enjoins us to use it with wisdom (Col 4:5). As we do, our Faithful Apologist, according to His own infinite wisdom, promises to draw people to Himself by persuading them of His glorious good news.

PART 1

BIBLICAL FOUNDATIONS
of Apologetics and Persuasion

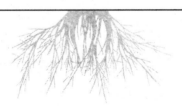

ONE

The DIVINE *Persuader*

Christianity is, and has always been, a religion of *persuasion*. If the core of persuasion is a *connection* between two (or more) different parties, then nowhere is this demonstrated more clearly than in God's activity as the Divine Persuader. We delight in the fact that, in history, the Lord God comes down and *speaks* directly to people. His words are given to His people because *He* stoops down to speak.

This may be so commonplace to us that we miss its majesty. It is, however, a glorious truth that the One who is infinite, eternal, and unchangeable, who Himself dwells in unapproachable light, nevertheless clothes Himself in such a way that we can see and know Him. It is the most remarkable truth of our Christian religion: The triune God, whom we otherwise could not approach, *approaches us* in order that we might come to Him and live with Him for eternity.

In Islam, to use just one example, words and commands were supposedly given by Allah to Muhammad, over a period of twenty-three (or so) years. They were then given from Muhammad to the followers of Islam. Debate still rages in Islam over whether the eternal Allah could even touch the temporal world to transmit the words of the Koran.[1] It is "below" Allah to be in touch with time. The Koran simply reveals Allah's will. It is not, nor could it be in any way, a "coming down" of Allah

---

1. For a discussion of Islam and Christianity, see K. Scott Oliphint, *Covenantal Apologetics: Principles and Practice in Defense of Our Faith* (Wheaton, IL: Crossway Books, 2013), 225–57.

3

himself. To come down is beneath Allah; it would mar and negate His transcendent character.

Not so with the true and triune God. Not only *does* He come down to us, but He does so without changing His glorious character in any way. The true God is not, so to speak, "imprisoned" by His character, as in Islam. Instead, He can express that character in time and space, without denying or negating it. This is the glory of God's condescension to us, centrally in His Son.

THE WORD OF CREATION

As we open our Bibles to the first few pages and sit back for a minute to consider what is happening in the garden as God speaks to Adam and Eve, we will recognize that what God is doing there is nothing short of remarkable and astonishing.

When we read those first words of Scripture, "In the beginning, God . . . ," we recognize that "the beginning" refers us to the beginning of *everything, except* God. "The beginning" is the beginning of all of creation. It is the beginning of time and space, of the heavens and the earth, of light and of darkness, of the waters and the living creatures that dwell in them, of the birds in the sky and the beasts of the field, and, climactically, of man—both male and female (Gen 1:1–31).

When we read those beginning words, we intuitively recognize that God is the one who brings about everything else that is. He is able to do so because, in the beginning, *He already was* (see John 1:1–3). In other words, the *reason* that everything in creation exists is because God, who always exists, brings everything in creation into existence. Those four simple words at the beginning of our Bibles—"In the beginning, God"— have enough content packed into them to occupy us for a lifetime.

The fact that God already exists "in the beginning" means that there is no cause to His existence. He simply *is* (Exod 3:14–16; Rev 4:8). The fact that He simply is includes the fact that God is not bound by, or in any way dependent on, that which He has created (Acts 17:24; Ps 115:3; 135:6). Because He *is* when everything else comes into existence by His own speech, everything that He speaks into existence is subject to Him, and not vice versa (Neh 9:6). He creates, and He is sovereign over all that He has made (Eph 1:11); and He has made everything (Rev 4:11).

The first thing we see when we open our Bibles, then, is that this God creates everything that is. The Bible tells us that God created the heavens and the earth. Because the earth was originally formless and empty, God began to give it shape and to fill it. The *way* in which God gave shape and fullness to His creation should cause us to pause. The entire first chapter of Genesis is filled with the reality of God *speaking* (Gen 1:3, 6, 9, 11, 20, 24, 26). Form and fullness were given to God's creation, in other words, by and through God's very *speech*. Why, we might ask, does God *speak* in order to form and fill His initially formless and empty creation?

It cannot be that God *had to* speak in order to form and to fill His universe. Since He is all-powerful, He could have formed and filled His creation simply by willing it to be. But instead, He *speaks* the form and fullness of creation into existence.

One of the reasons God speaks the form and fullness of creation into existence is to show us, His readers, that He is, in the first place, a God who will condescend to *communicate* to and in His creation. That is, He is not a God who cannot and does not relate to His creation, who stands far off, as it were, and simply *wills* it into existence, ensuring all along that He will not in any way be "touched" by what He has made. From the beginning, God is a *communicating* God, a speaking God, a talking God. From His lofty, infinite, and eternal heights, He comes, and He speaks.

On the sixth day, and immediately after creating man—male and female—in His image, He condescends to speak to them. He tells them— person to person, as it were—what it is that they are created to do:

> God blessed them and said to them, "Be fruitful and increase in number; fill the earth and subdue it. Rule over the fish in the sea and the birds in the sky and over every living creature that moves on the ground."

Then God said, "I give you every seed-bearing plant on the face of the whole earth and every tree that has fruit with seed in it. They will be yours for food. And to all the beasts of the earth and all the birds in the sky and all the creatures that move along the ground—everything that has the breath of life in it—I give every green plant for food." And it was so. (Gen 1:28–30)

As we come to the creation of Adam and Eve, it is "natural" that God would continue to speak. He has been speaking all along. In the account of the creation of creatures made in His image, He speaks first to Himself as He contemplates what it means to create human beings in His image (Gen 1:26). This moment, we should see, is a significant shift in the five-day rhythm of God's creative activity. Prior to this, God simply spoke, and it was. But now, on the sixth day, we're told that God communicates with Himself. Why this shift?

Surely one reason for the shift is to indicate to us that God is about to do something in His creation that is wholly unique, something with substantial and eternal consequences. To this point, all that He has created could pass away, including heaven and earth itself. The first five days of creation were, we could say, "God's days." They brought about things in the world that had no intrinsic eternal longevity. God could, of course, preserve them as long as He saw fit. Creation, up to day five, could glorify God for as long as God chose to keep it in existence. But there was nothing *in* creation on those first five days that *required* that its existence, now begun, would never cease.

On day six, everything changed. God takes counsel with Himself because, as we will see later from Scripture, the decision to create people in His image will mean that what is made will endure for eternity (e.g., Matt 25:41–46; John 17:3). It is almost as if the triune God is saying to Himself on day six, "Are we sure that we want to create something in our image, so that we will live eternally with them?" This, obviously, was a decision of great moment, of great *eternal* moment; it was a decision fundamentally different from everything else God had thus far decided to create.

All of this, of course, is given to us in Scripture to highlight the climax of God's creation as He creates Adam from the dust, and Eve from Adam. Once God commits Himself to create something in His image, He commits Himself to a *relationship* that will never end, a relationship with creatures of His who will, in a created and dependent way, be *like Him*.

Light and darkness could not be like Him; sea creatures and birds could not be like Him; livestock and creeping things and beasts could not be like Him. For sure, all that He had made through day five would give abundant testimony to who He is and what He is like (see Ps 19:1–5; Rom 1:20). But nothing thus far could *image* His own, personal character. Since God Himself is *personal* as Father, Son, and Holy Spirit, He communicates and has fellowship with Himself according to His personal character, including His mind and will. Through day five of creation, nothing personal has been created. With the creation of Adam, there was now a Person-to-person relationship.

So, God commits Himself to an eternal relationship with those made to be like Him. He creates creatures whose purpose is to *image* or *show* what God Himself is like. He creates creatures who could think, who could make decisions, who could communicate to each other with words, who could rule over other aspects of God's creation. He creates creatures who, for the first time in this process, have the very "breath of life" breathed into them by God, so that by that breath they became "living beings" (Gen 2:7).

The point is that the "living beings" they became were wholly different than the creatures that were previously created. None of the other creatures made were made alive by virtue of God's own in-breathing. Man—male and female—alone was a product of God's own breath. He alone was distinct and set apart by God among all else that God had made. This will be a significant point to remember as we move forward in our discussion of persuasion and apologetics.

God then spoke to those made in His image and told them why they were placed in His creation. Unlike the rest of creation that God had spoken into existence, those made in His image were given commands that only image-bearers could fulfill. Like others in creation, they were told to be fruitful and multiply. But, unlike the rest of creation, they were told to rule over the rest of what God had made. And they were told from what trees they could eat, and from which tree they should not eat. They were given, under God, *responsibility* to obey God in His garden. It was a responsibility that, unlike anything else created, would carry substantial consequences.

The first thing we see "in the beginning," then, is that God does not simply create from afar. Instead, in the process of forming and filling that which He has created, He introduces the *means* by which He Himself will *relate* to His creation. He *speaks* to and into His creation. And, as this process reaches its high point on day six, He speaks to those made in His image. In that speaking, He has initiated a relationship with our first parents, and through them, with us. That relationship is initiated *because* God, who communicates by speaking, also gives to His image the gift of speech (Gen 2:19–20, 23).

It is crucial for us to see the depth of this truth. God's own sovereign and wise choice for "connecting" Himself to His creation was, first of all, by way of *speech*. And His own sovereign and wise way of "connecting" Himself to those made in His image was by speaking to them as those who could respond, *by speaking. Speech*, in other words, is the first "bridge" God institutes to connect to us; *it is the first God-initiated and God-ordained mode of persuasion.* Our tendency, perhaps, is to take language for granted. Children learn it simply by getting older and watching their parents and others around them speak. It appears to be effortless and natural for them. For most children, the complexities of language do not hinder them. They simply "adapt" to speaking.

But language has an incomprehensible quality about it. It distinguishes human beings from the rest of creation. The mathematical genius Kurt Gödel (1906–78) once quipped, "The more I think about language the more it amazes me that people even understand each other."[2] This is

2. Rebecca Goldstein, *Incompleteness: The Proof and Paradox of Kurt Gödel* (New York: W. W. Norton and Co., 2005), 110.

exactly right. That we have been created to utter sounds in such a way that it reaches other human beings and provides understanding is, in the end, like the God who speaks, incomprehensible to us.

This initial connection, through speech and language, is initially a gift from God. It is a gift to be used for His glory. So strong is this "word-connection," that, after the fall into sin, people began to see it as a point of pride:

> Now the whole world had one language and a common speech. As people moved eastward, they found a plain in Shinar and settled there. They said to each other, "Come, let's make bricks and bake them thoroughly." They used brick instead of stone, and tar for mortar. Then they said, "Come, let us build ourselves a city, with a tower that reaches to the heavens, so that we may make a name for ourselves; otherwise we will be scattered over the face of the whole earth." (Gen 11:1–4)

The gift of speech became a stumbling block for people; it had the potential of creating a mighty monument of pride and self-assurance, against the Lord who had given them that gift in the first place (Gen 11:6). The very thing the Lord made to connect us to Him, was now, after the fall, being used to try to usurp His Lordship. The gift became a curse.

The Lord had to break that universal connection of language so that sinful people would not rise up as *one voice* in their pride against Him. He had to confuse that universal language. The "connection" that language provided for all people now became a series of "disconnections," as people were scattered according to their language differences.

We see in the New Testament that this confusion of languages begins to be undone on the day of Pentecost. On that day, the Lord gives gifts of languages (i.e., tongues) so that the communication of the gospel is not hindered by all the disparate languages (Acts 2:5–12). The Lord ensures, in the preaching of the gospel, that a language connection would be re-established. Persuasion through language would continue throughout the world as the gospel is proclaimed to all people.

The point of the Babel/Pentecost example is that language is a powerful, perhaps the *most* powerful, means of connection that the Lord has made. If we recognize that persuasion includes a *connection* between two (or more) people, *speech* is the initial, powerful "bridge" that God used and uses to *connect* Himself to us, and to connect us to each other. He did not have to speak at all; God does not need any particular means whatsoever to do what He does. But He chose to speak; He condescended to use words, even as Adam and Eve could themselves respond to Him by using words.

The Lord created creatures who could both hear Him and speak to Him. So powerful is this gift of speech, that we should recognize as well that the serpent used God's gift of language as the means by which to tempt, confuse, and potentially destroy Adam and Eve.

And with that speech, from and to God, there is a God-designed and God-initiated "link" between those made in His image and God Himself. Without that God-ordained "link," He might have remained in unapproachable light; we may not have known Him at all, nor connected with Him. That which is limited, changeable, and temporal is intrinsically unable to touch that which is infinite, immutable, and eternal. There is no "link" to God unless He first comes down and connects Himself to us. And this "coming down" had its initial focus in God's very words.

THE WORD OF THE LORD

As we recognize from the rest of Scripture, God speaking was not simply a random or arbitrary choice He made, as if He had pondered various ways He might relate to us and picked one at random. There is a much richer and deeper reason that God used words "in the beginning" of creation. God relating to us and communicating to us using *words* points us to *the Word Himself,* the one who would come down in history to show us who God is, and to persuade us, in and through His word, to come to Him.

The apostle John, as he pens his Gospel under the inspiration of the Holy Spirit, immediately refers us back to those first three words of Scripture, "In the beginning": "In the beginning was the Word, and the Word was with God, and the Word was God" (John 1:1).

In referring us back to the beginning, however, he also highlights for us another, primary reason that God uses words to communicate. He uses words, because it is of His very character, as the one who is *with* God and who *is* God, to *be* the Word. John turns our attention to the second person of the Trinity—the Word Himself. He is the one who was there, in the beginning. John tells us that it is the *Word* Himself, the second person of the Trinity, who was "in the beginning with God."

Not only so, but it is through this Word that all things were made, and "without him nothing was made that has been made. In him was life, and that life was the light of all mankind" (John 1:3–4). In other words, it was the Word Himself through whom God the Father (together with the Holy Spirit; see Gen 1:2) created the universe. One of the reasons that God *speaks* creation into existence is because it is through *the Word* that creation comes to be. God communicating and speaking to creation, and climactically to Adam and Eve, points us to the Word, without whom "was not any thing made that was made" (John 1:3 ESV).

As John writes his Gospel, the Greek word that he uses for "Word"—*Logos*—already had a long philosophical pedigree. The pre-Socratic philosopher, Heraclitus (535–475 BC), taught that the *Logos* was the one, unchanging aspect to an ever-changing reality. He also believed that the *Logos* was intricately connected to human speech, since it was through speech that we can understand truth.

Philo of Alexandria (20 BC–50 AD), a Hellenistic Jew, incorporated substantial aspects of Greek philosophy into his Jewish theology. He saw the *Logos* as the primary organizing principle of philosophy and of theology, since it was the *Logos* that provided a connecting link between the transcendent God and His creation. These philosophical uses of the notion of *Logos* are variously related to John's use of that word in Scripture. As we will see in part 2, the notion of *Logos* plays a significant role in persuasion as well.

The Holy Spirit was fully aware of (even as He Himself had ordained) the philosophical connotations that the word *Logos* carried as He inspired John to write. But we should not think that it was the *philosophical* use of the concept of *Logos* that was paramount in its use and its meaning in John. There is a use of the notion of *Logos* that goes back further and is more intricately linked than the various philosophical uses of the word in John's day. There is a much more striking (and, to some extent, underappreciated) use of the word that has its roots in the Old Testament.[3]

One of the phrases that occurs frequently in the Old Testament, especially in connection with the prophets, is the phrase "and the word of the Lord came." As a matter of fact, that (or a similar) phrase occurs 103 times in the Old Testament. But it is instructive to us to note carefully how the phrase is often worded.

For example, the first place that we see this phrase is in Genesis 15:1: "After this, the word of the LORD came to Abram in a vision: 'Do not be afraid, Abram. I am your shield, your very great reward.'" If we pause for a minute, we should notice something very telling in this verse. Moses tells us here that "the word of the LORD came to Abram." Our initial thought might be that Abram simply heard *words* that came to him from the Lord. We might think this would be similar to someone writing us a letter, and we would say, "A letter from my mother came to me."

But there are clues here that might move our thinking in a different direction. What we're actually told is that "the word of the LORD came to Abram *in a vision*." What could that mean? Of course, it *could* mean that Abram actually saw the *words* that came to him by way of a vision. This would be analogous to someone saying, "a letter of my mother came to me in a vision."

But the grammar here might actually lean in a different direction. Even if I could see my mother's letter in a vision, I would more likely say

---

3. The same word, *Logos*, was not used in the Old Testament since the Old Testament was written in Hebrew (and Aramaic), and not in Greek. However, since the same Holy Spirit who inspired the writing of the New Testament also inspired the writing of the Old Testament, language differences are no obstacle to the unity of meaning between the two Testaments.

something like, "A letter from my mother appeared to me in a vision." To say a letter *of* my mother *came* to me seems to be an odd way of speaking.

It is possible, given the way this is phrased, that the word of the Lord that came to Abram in a vision was a *person* who Himself spoke the words that Abram heard that day. The notion that some*one came* to Abram is consistent with the biblical idea that the word of the Lord was *sent* to Abram. The vision, in other words, that Abram saw that day might have been a vision of a person who spoke the Lord's words to Abram. Consistent with this idea is the fact that the person speaking was Himself the *Word* of the Lord, who was sent, and who came and spoke.

Some of what we see in this passage with Abram becomes clearer to us as we move through the Old Testament. Looking at more of these kinds of passages that tell us "the word of the Lord came" begins to show us more clearly how we might want to think about them.

For example, if we pay attention to the way "the word of the Lord" is used in various ways in 1 Samuel 3:1, we can't help but notice how it could point us to the Word Himself:

> The boy Samuel ministered before the Lord under Eli. In those days the word of the Lord was rare; *there were not many visions* (emphasis mine).

> Now Samuel did not yet know the Lord: *The word of the Lord had not yet been revealed to him* (3:7, emphasis mine).

> The Lord continued to appear at Shiloh, and there *he revealed himself to Samuel through his word* (3:21, emphasis mine).

These passages indicate that "the word of the Lord" was inextricably linked to *visions* and *revelations* to Samuel. Perhaps this could mean that what Samuel was meant to see, and what was revealed to him, were *words* that would express to Samuel what he needed to know. It is telling that we are told that the word of the Lord was rare, *not* because the Lord was not *speaking*, but rather because *visions* were rare.

We see again here a link between the word of the Lord and a vision. It may very well be that this means a vision *of the Lord*. It is all the more likely, however, given 3:21 above. There we read that the Lord revealed Himself *through His word*. This clause, "through His word" is the *means* the Lord used to reveal Himself.

Thus, "the word of the Lord" could be a personal revelation or vision from God to Samuel; the Lord reveals *Himself* through *the word* of the Lord. These verses in 1 Samuel 3 lead us to conclude that what Samuel eventually received from the Lord was a revelation of the Lord Himself, which could be the person who is *the Word* of the Lord.

In 1 Kings 19, we notice a passage that seems intent on pointing us to a "person-to-person" revelation of "the word of the LORD." Of Elijah, we read, "There he went into a cave and spent the night. And the word of the LORD came to him: 'What are you doing here, Elijah?'" (1 Kgs 19:9). Here it looks like "the word of the LORD" is a person who spoke to Elijah in that cave. The English Standard Version (ESV) translates a clause from the Hebrew that the NIV left out, and thus, shows this more clearly: "And behold, the word of the LORD came to him, *and he said to him*, 'What are you doing here, Elijah?'" (ESV, emphasis mine). According to this translation, the word of the Lord that came to Elijah is actually one ("He") who spoke to him.

While time and space prevent us from reviewing the rest of the 103 passages in the Old Testament that refer to the word of the Lord, if we did, we would see this pattern of personification continue. Before we move on, however, we need to notice another biblical passage that helps us recognize the possibility that "the word of the Lord" might be more personal than linguistic. The call of Jeremiah the prophet provides some clarity about the possible identity of this "Word":

The word of the LORD came to me, saying, "Before I formed you in the womb I knew you, before you were born I set you apart; I appointed you as a prophet to the nations." "Alas, Sovereign LORD," I said, "I do not know how to speak; I am too young." But the LORD said to me,

"Do not say, 'I am too young.' You must go to everyone I send you to and say whatever I command you. Do not be afraid of them, for I am with you and will rescue you," declares the LORD. *Then the LORD reached out his hand and touched my mouth* and said to me, "I have put my words in your mouth." (Jer 1:4–9)

Again we see that "the word of the LORD" came, and *He* spoke. This "coming" and "speaking" rules out any idea that what came to Jeremiah was a group of words from the Lord. That which came to Jeremiah *came and spoke*. No inanimate letter could do such a thing. This points us to the possibility of a *personal* manifestation of the Lord Himself, who is present to interact with, and to call, Jeremiah as a prophet.

As a matter of fact, just after "the word of the LORD" speaks to Jeremiah, he immediately responds, "Alas, Sovereign LORD!"[4] This "word of the LORD" who came to Jeremiah and who spoke is Himself, as Jeremiah recognizes, *the Lord God*. There is a seamless transition in the text from "the word of the Lord" who is there and who is speaking to Jeremiah, and Jeremiah's addressing Him as the Sovereign Lord Himself.

In this one passage we have identified for us one who is both "the word of the Lord" and who, according to Jeremiah, is the Lord God. If we think about this, we can see that it begins to sound uncannily similar to what we have already seen in John 1:1! The one who is the Word, and who is "with God," is Himself God, who has come down, as the Word, to be with us.

Even more telling and astounding in this passage, especially as we have John 1 in mind, is that the One who is there speaking to Jeremiah, who is initially described as "the word of the Lord," and also as "the Sovereign Lord," also *puts out His hand and touches Jeremiah's mouth*. It seems altogether likely that this "word of the Lord" has come to speak to Jeremiah *in the form of a man* and is standing there to call Jeremiah to his prophetic task, *person to person*.

---

4. The Hebrew is "Adonai Yahweh," which can also be translated "the Lord God."

This points us to *the* Word Himself, the second person of the Trinity. Here we see one who is *both* "the word of the Lord" *and* who is also "the Lord God." He is "of the Lord" as one who came and who was sent from God, and He is the Lord God Himself. Here is the One who *was* "in the beginning," who was both *with* God, and who *was* God. There is a "from-ness" of this One who is "of the Lord," as well as an identity, since He *is* the Lord. He is the word *of* the Lord, who Himself *is* the Lord.

As we read these many occasions in the Old Testament when "the word of the Lord" comes to various people at different times and places, we should recognize that they are pointing us to the One who would climactically condescend "when the set time had fully come" (Gal 4:4). These numerous passages are meant to thrust our thinking forward as we recognize that this word of the Lord who came and spoke and interacted with so many in the Old Testament, is likely the very same Word— the *Logos*—who became flesh in order to dwell among us *as one of us* (John 1:14).

We will remember that our working definition of persuasion is the discerning and initiating of a *connection* between two or more persons. In this case, a connection is initiated between the triune God and human beings. This connection, we should recognize, is unlike any other. It is unique, because it is between One who is infinite, eternal, and unchangeable, and human beings who are finite, temporal, and ever changing. If there was to be *any* communication and connection at all, God Himself would have to build the bridge between Himself and us. And that's exactly what He did, in most remarkable ways. He did that, by "coming down," as it were, to His creation. He did that, by speaking in human language. He did that, climactically, by becoming *one of us*! Thus, there is an inextricable link between the *speech* of God, the *Word* of God, and persuasion. God *persuades* us centrally through His speech, His Word, the second person of the Trinity.

Although the Lord's ultimate and climactic act of persuasion was the miracle of the incarnation, that miracle had persuasive precursors prior to it. In other words, even as the Lord personally and gloriously became one of us in the Son, He also personally and gloriously hinted at His incarnation throughout redemptive history.

It may help to see examples of this, as the Old Testament points us to that climactic event of the incarnation of the second person of the Trinity in the New Testament. On a number of occasions, the Old Testament uses the phrase "the angel of the Lord." In fact, we see this phrase in the Old Testament a total of fifty-six times. One of the first times it is used is when the Lord is dealing with Hagar:

> The angel of the Lord found Hagar near a spring in the desert; it was the spring that is beside the road to Shur. And he said, "Hagar, slave of Sarai, where have you come from, and where are you going?" "I'm running away from my mistress Sarai," she answered. Then the angel of the Lord told her, "Go back to your mistress and submit to her." The angel added, "I will increase your descendants so much that they will be too numerous to count." The angel of the Lord also said to her: "You are now pregnant and you will give birth to a son. You shall name him Ishmael, for the Lord has heard of your misery. He will be a wild donkey of a man; his hand will be against everyone and everyone's hand against him, and he will live in hostility toward all his brothers." She gave this name to the Lord who spoke to her: "You are the God who sees me," for she said, "I have now seen the One who sees me." (Gen 16:7–13)

Notice what this angel is doing here. First, He gives a promise to Hagar that only the Lord Himself could give. He says to her, "I will surely multiply your offspring . . ." Whatever we might understand about angels from Scripture, we can certainly recognize that angels do not have the power or prerogative to promise what only God Himself can accomplish.

It should not surprise us, then, when we read that Hagar "gave this name to *the Lord who spoke to her* . . ." Hagar knew to whom she had spoken. She called it "You are *the God* who sees me." This "angel of the

Lord" was no mere angel who appeared to Hagar. The angel of the Lord who came to Hagar is the One who was sent (which is what "angel" means), and is the Lord Himself, and Hagar knew it. This is the second person of the Trinity, the Word, the Son Himself.

In that familiar passage in Exodus 3 when the Lord appeared to Moses in a burning bush to call him to his task, we see the same interplay between the angel of the Lord who is the Lord:

> There the angel of the LORD appeared to him in flames of fire from within a bush. Moses saw that though the bush was on fire it did not burn up. So Moses thought, "I will go over and see this strange sight—why the bush does not burn up." When the LORD saw that he had gone over to look, God called to him from within the bush, "Moses! Moses!" And Moses said, "Here I am." "Do not come any closer," God said. "Take off your sandals, for the place where you are standing is holy ground." Then he said, "I am the God of your father, the God of Abraham, the God of Isaac and the God of Jacob." At this, Moses hid his face, because he was afraid to look at God. (Exod 3:2–6)

We see here again, initially, that "the angel of the LORD" appears to Moses. Immediately after identifying this one who appeared as "the angel of the LORD," we read that "*the* LORD saw that he turned aside" and then "*God* called to him" (ESV, emphasis mine).

Again, with no indication that there is more than one person speaking from the burning bush, Scripture tells us that Moses is dealing with "the angel of the LORD" who is "the LORD" and is identified as "God." It is abundantly clear here that the Lord Himself, the "I am who I am," is present here. This is why Moses is commanded to take off his sandals. Only the presence of the Lord could sanctify and set apart the place where Moses stands. No mere angel can sanctify the earth with His presence. Moses is face-to-face with the Lord on this mountain.

In his discussion of this passage in Exodus 3, the Puritan John Owen (1616–83), draws together these same threads:

And herein also have we expressed *another glorious appearance of the Son of God.* He who is here revealed is called *"Jehovah,"* verse 4; and he affirms of himself that he is "the God of Abraham," verse 6; who also describes himself by the glorious name of *"I am that I am,"* verse 14; in whose name and authority Moses dealt with Pharaoh in the deliverance of the people, and whom they were to serve on that mountain upon their coming out of Egypt; . . . And yet he is expressly called an "Angel," Exod. 3:2,—namely, the Angel of the covenant, the great Angel of the presence of God, *in whom was the name and nature of God.* And he thus appeared that the church might know and consider who it was that was to work out their spiritual and eternal salvation, whereof that deliverance which then he would effect was a type and pledge. . . . and *this was no other but the Son of God.*[5]

Owen here reiterates for us the identity of this one who is the "angel of the Lord." He is the Lord Himself, *Yahweh,* the "I Am," even as He is the one who is sent by God to Moses. He is the second person of the Trinity, the Word of God.

This pattern of the "angel of the Lord" who is sent by God, *and who is the Lord,* is repeated numerous times throughout the Old Testament. Is it any wonder, then, that Jesus reminded His hearers, on more than one occasion, that the entire Old Testament spoke of, and pointed to, *Him* (see, for example, John 5:39, 46; Luke 24:27)? Surely, the Lord had been condescending to people in order, personally and persuasively, to *connect* with them throughout redemptive history. The Lord's own "mode" of persuasion includes not only His *words* and *speech* to His human creatures. He also "comes down" to them as He speaks and acts in order to reveal Himself. Like a parent who stoops down to speak to a young child using the child's still-infantile sounds and words, the Lord "stoops down" to our level and speaks to us, connecting to us, in order that we might have communion with Him.

---

5. John Owen, "An Exposition of the Epistle to the Hebrews," ed. W. H. Goold, vol. 18, *Works of John Owen* (Edinburgh: Johnstone and Hunter, 1854), 225–26 (emphases mine).

THE IMAGE OF THE INVISIBLE GOD

There is one more connecting link between (the Son of) God and us that should be highlighted here. We noted above that when God created man—male and female—He determined to create them "in His image." There is much that can be said about "the image of God," and we will return to this point later on. Not only has the Son of God condescended, throughout redemptive history, in order to connect Himself with us, but we should also recognize another central truth about the second person of the Trinity that Scripture teaches us.

We have now seen that the Son is the *Logos*, the Word of God Himself. We have also seen that the Old Testament speaks of "the word of the Lord" in a way that may point to the Lord Himself. And we have seen that the "angel of the Lord" in the Old Testament is often the One who is both *sent*, and who is Himself the Lord. What these things reveal, then, is that there is One who is both distinct from God and who is also identical to God.

The different ways in which this One is described—as the Word, as an Angel—causes us to recognize that there is a "from-ness" of this One who is the Lord. Just as a word implies a speaker of that word, so also One who is *the* Word is *from* the One who speaks.

Viewing this with New Testament eyes, we can now see that this points us to the reality that the Son, who is Himself fully God (John 1:1; 8:58) is also, at the same time, the One who, as the Word, reveals to us the "speaker" of that Word. The Son came to do the Father's bidding, even as He alone is uniquely capable of showing us the Father (see, for example, Matt 11:27; Luke 22:29; John 5:17–37; 6:27, 46; 8:18, 28, 54; 10:18, 29, 37; 14:9–12, 20; 15:1, 26; 18:11; 20:17, 21).

In line with this "from-ness" of the Son (as the Word from the Speaker, as the Angel who is sent), Scripture also designates the identity of the Son as the "image" of the invisible God. Note, in speaking of the beloved Son (v. 14), Scripture gives us this description of Him:

The Son is the image of the invisible God, the firstborn over all creation. For in him all things were created: things in heaven and on earth, visible and invisible, whether thrones or powers or rulers or authorities; all things have been created through him and for him. He is before all things, and in him all things hold together. (Col 1:15–17)

There is in this passage, no doubt, a confirmation that Christ came in the flesh to show us the "invisible God." But we should not miss the fact that this "image" character of the Son is tied to the fact that "in him all things were created . . ." In other words, there is a close link between what we have seen in John 1:1–3, which affirms the creative activity of the Word, and what we see here in Colossians.

The same kind of relation of the "from-ness" of the Son is expressed in Hebrews 1. In that chapter, the author begins by confirming, from the Old Testament, the fact that the Son Himself is fully God. Thus, he begins with this description of Him:

The Son is the radiance of God's glory and the exact representation of his being, sustaining all things by his powerful word. After he had provided purification for sins, he sat down at the right hand of the Majesty in heaven. (Heb 1:3)

Notice, the Son is the "radiance" and the "exact representation" of God's very being. Both ways of describing Him—a "radiance" and a "representation"—indicate a "from-ness" of the Son. But, lest we think that this "from-ness" would make Him less than fully God, the author leaves no doubt about the Son's deity:

And again, when God brings his firstborn into the world, he says, "Let all God's angels worship him." In speaking of the angels he says, "He makes his angels spirits, and his servants flames of fire." But about the Son he says, "Your throne, O God, will last for ever and ever; a scepter

of justice will be the scepter of your kingdom. You have loved righteousness and hated wickedness; therefore God, your God, has set you above
your companions by anointing you with the oil of joy." (Heb 1:6–9)

Any Hebrew who knew the Old Testament, as the original recipients
of this letter would have, would readily see that this One who is the
"radiance" of God's glory and the "exact representation of His being" is,
Himself, *fully* God.

There could be no other explanation for the command (applied to the
Son) that the angels were meant to *worship* Him. As the author applies
Psalm 45 to the Son, he says, "Your throne, O *God*, will last forever and
ever . . ." To command worship of the Son, and to apply the throne of the
Old Testament, which is God's alone, to Him would be nothing short of
blasphemy, unless the Son was fully God.

As we see the apostle Paul, under the inspiration of the Holy Spirit,
writing in Colossians 1 of the Son *as image*, then, we should see again that
this is a unique ascription of the Son that both recognizes His "from-ness"
in relation to the Father, but also affirms His full and absolute deity.
Indeed, the fact that He is, eternally and infinitely, *the Son*, points us
immediately to His Father, and helps us see that while each is fully and
completely God, the Father is uniquely the one from whom the Son is,
and the Son is uniquely from the Father.

As we recognize the Son as the eternal "image of God," we can see
a bit more clearly, perhaps, one of the reasons why the triune God determined to create Adam and Eve, and their posterity, in God's *image*. The
creation of human beings in the image of God was, in part, God's way of
"connecting" us, in a wholly unique way, with Himself. More specifically,
as the image of God, human beings are "linked" to the One who is the
eternal, infinite, and glorious "*image* of the invisible God"—the Son of
God Himself.

The fascinating and intricate theological details that could be
pursued in this regard are multifaceted. Without moving too far afield,
a couple of quotations at this point are instructive. First, the Puritan

Matthew Henry (1662–1714), speaking of Adam and Eve in the garden, just after their sin, says:

> Observe here, what was the cause and occasion of their fear; they heard the voice of the Lord God walking in the garden in the cool of the day. It was the approach of the Judge, that put them into a fright and yet he came in such a manner, as made it formidable only to guilty consciences. *It is supposed that he came in a human shape*, and that he who judged the world now, was the same that shall judge the world at the last day, even that man whom God has ordained: he appeared to them now, (it should seem,) *in no other similitude than that in which they had seen him when he put them into paradise*; for he came to convince and humble them, not to amaze and terrify them.[6]

Note what Henry says here. It was the Judge, the Son of God, who came to Adam and Eve in Genesis 3, walking in the garden, coming to judge them. He came in human form and, according to Henry, it was this same One, in the same form, who put Adam and Eve into paradise. In other words, Henry is recognizing that, since the Son is *from* the Father, since He is the One who is *sent*, since He is the One who permanently takes on a human nature at the incarnation, it was *He* who came to Adam and Eve, in a temporary human form, "in the beginning." The persuasion of God's speech, in other words, has always had its focus in the Son, who is the Word, the Angel, the Image of the invisible God.

Similarly, the Puritan Thomas Goodwin (1600–1680), in defending the title of the "Word" with respect to the Son, understands Genesis 1 like this:

> When I came to the creation, as in Gen. 1, from whence this title [i.e., Word] is given him, as by comparing John and Moses appears,

---

6. Matthew Henry, *An Exposition of the Old and New Testament*, ed. G. Burder and J. Hughes, vol. 1, (Philadelphia: E. Barrington and G. D. Haswell, 1828), 41 (emphases mine).

I considered, whether God, by a word within himself, did speak it as in *corde* (in the heart). Now so he had said, "Let there be light," and that from everlasting; and therefore why may we not suppose it to have been uttered at the beginning of every day's work? *And that voice being a creature, whether that clothing with words at creation, shewed not that Christ was to be clothed on with a creature, to speak God's mind unto us creatures,* and that he had so undertaken, as being that Wisdom who had sustained it in God's purpose, and now appeared to execute it.[7]

For Goodwin, it was the Word Himself who took on a human voice in order to speak to God's human creatures in the beginning. That act, in Genesis, according to Goodwin, looks forward to the time, after and because of the fall, when the Word would permanently unite Himself to our human nature. In that union of natures, the eternal "Image" unites with the created image. In that union, persuasion reaches its historical climax.

Now we should ask what it is that this Angel, this Word, this Image, this Son, this one who is Jesus Christ, came to reveal. Did He come only to reveal Himself?

As we have already mentioned, Jesus defined His own ministry in the context of His Father. For example, amid intense opposition and rejection from so many (Matt 11:18–24), Jesus turns to His Father with these words:

At that time Jesus said, "I praise you, Father, Lord of heaven and earth, because you have hidden these things from the wise and learned, and revealed them to little children. Yes, Father, for this is what you were pleased to do." (Matt 11:25–26)

Amid many rejections, Jesus turns to His Father with thanksgiving, because He sees that rejection in light of His Father's sovereign plan.

---

7. Thomas Goodwin, *The Works of Thomas Goodwin*, ed. Thomas Smith, vol. 4 (Edinburgh: James Nichol, 1863), 551 (emphasis mine).

But then Jesus makes a statement that could easily serve as a summary of His entire messianic ministry:

> All things have been committed to me by my Father. No one knows the Son except the Father, and no one knows the Father except the Son and those to whom the Son chooses to reveal him. (Matt 11:27)

This statement is as clear a declaration of Jesus's own divine identity in relation to His Father as any in Scripture. In this statement, Jesus claims exclusive knowledge of His heavenly Father, and that knowledge is reciprocated by His Father.

What Jesus says here (and it appears that He is speaking to His disciples at this point) is that whatever His Father has planned, whatever He has willed, has been handed over to Him, as the Messiah, the one who was sent to do the Father's will. In handing all things over to Jesus the Messiah, the Father has given His Son the authority and prerogative of choosing to reveal to whomever He wishes the knowledge of the Father and the Son.

This is a momentous statement in the life and ministry of Christ. It defines Christ's ministry as both *from* the Father, whom the Son alone knows intimately, and *to* His people, for whom eternal life is to know the Father and the Son (John 17:3). He is the "connection" between the Father and us. Is it any wonder, then, given what Jesus has said here to His disciples, that we sense His frustration toward Philip in the upper room?

> Philip said, "Lord, show us the Father and that will be enough for us." Jesus answered: "Don't you know me, Philip, even after I have been among you such a long time? Anyone who has seen me has seen the Father. How can you say, 'Show us the Father'? Don't you believe that I am in the Father, and that the Father is in me? The words I say to you I do not speak on my own authority. Rather, it is the Father, living in me, who is doing his work. Believe me when I say that I am in the Father and the Father is in me; or at least believe on the evidence of the works themselves." (John 14:8–11)

Unless we recognize that the One who, from the beginning, was *sent and* came to reveal to us both Himself and His Father (through the Holy Spirit; see, for example, Matt 1:18, 20; 3:16; 12:18, 28), we miss the depth and scope of the ministry of the Son. Not only so, but we miss the Lord's own design of divine persuasion.

His was a Trinitarian ministry, from the beginning. It was a ministry designed, from eternity past, so that the One sent would, "when the set time had fully come" (Gal 4:4), reveal Himself and His Father, through the Spirit, to those who would repent and believe, according to God's sovereign plan.

We may have forgotten by this point why it is important to highlight the identity of this "word of the Lord," this "angel of the Lord," this "image of the invisible God," this "Word," in the Old Testament and into the New.

It began, we will remember, with God Himself *speaking* creation into existence. That speaking of God in those six days reached its climax in His speaking to Adam and Eve, and since they alone were made in His image, *they could speak back to Him*. The connection, the link, between God and His human creatures was, in the first place, a connection of the *word*, of speech. God's own condescension, by which He establishes a relationship to Adam and Eve, is, initially, a condescension of the *word*.

We then noted that this *Word*, by which the Lord condescends, is in the first place, the second person of the Trinity. This is John's point as he begins to write his Gospel. The "Word" that is *from God* is, first of all, not a linguistic phenomenon, but is, in the first place, a *person*, the person of the Son of God.

The apostle John, no doubt because he would have known the Scriptures (our Old Testament) so well, would have recognized that this *Logos* who is the Son of God is the same one who was active and appearing throughout redemptive history. He was the one who would appear, temporarily and on occasion, in the form of a man, in order to show to the saints of the Old Testament that He would one day come, finally and climactically, both to reveal who God is, and to save His people from their sins (Matt 1:21).

The one whose name would be Emmanuel, God with us, is the same one who was "God with us" in the Old Testament as well. When He permanently took on a human nature, His status as Emmanuel was permanently put in place, from that time into eternity. From that time forward, the dwelling place of God would be with us, supremely so in the new heavens and the new earth (see John 14:23; Rev 21:3).

The importance of language can hardly be overestimated as a means of connection and thus of persuasion. Anyone who has traveled to a foreign country recognizes the crucial need to communicate in the same language whenever possible. Any parent, to use another example, knows it is sometimes best to condescend to speak simple language with a child in order to communicate.

But think of how much more effective it would be if, in a foreign country, for example, you could become *one of them*. Instead of entering that country as a native of your own, imagine the connection you could make if you suddenly became one of their own. Or, as a parent, imagine how you could more effectively communicate with and persuade your child if you could actually become like him. This, we should see, is exactly what the Lord Himself has done. Not only has He personally and perpetually *spoken* to us, but He has, in the Son, *become one of us* in order to draw us to Himself.

The Lord God, who is all-powerful and who can do whatever He pleases, might have connected with us in any number of ways. Our minds are too feeble and short-sighted to understand what is possible for Him. He sovereignly chose, however, to connect with us *by appearing as, and eventually becoming, one of us*, even as He remains who He eternally is. Truly, this is the ultimate act of persuasion; the Son of God became one of us!

Again, the god of Islam *could not* do such a thing; it would be seen to be beneath him. But the true God—Father, Son, and Holy Spirit—is fully able to become one of us, in the person of the Son, without in any way giving up or denying who and what He is as God. This is a remarkable truth. It is a truth that no one else has even imagined (1 Cor 2:9). It is a truth that no other religion can even approach. It is the glorious and majestic truth of God's condescension to us.

That condescension, we can now see, is God's utter, and finally incomprehensible, *way of persuasion*; it is God's way of drawing people to Himself. He comes to us—*sent* as the Angel; *speaking* as the Word; *revealing* as the Image—and He communicates to us the glory of the triune God in the gospel. He does this, not simply by *speaking*, as wonderful as that is, but by coming down to us and speaking *as one of us* (Heb 1:1–2).

The spoken word "in the beginning" is the "Word of the Lord" in redemptive history, and is the "Word made flesh" in the New Testament. From the beginning, God connects Himself to us through the Word. He connects Himself to us, and in so doing He changes hearts that oppose Him to hearts that long to please Him. Our triune God is, and has been from the beginning, a God of glorious *persuasion*, from the Father, through the Son, and in the Spirit.

As we consider the importance of persuasion, especially as it relates to our defense of Christianity, we only properly consider it when we see the triune God as the initiator and sustainer of persuasion. He *spoke* in order to connect Himself to us. He spoke in and by His Word, the second person of the Trinity, apart from whom there can be no proper connection to God. Persuasion begins with the triune God—Father, Son, and Holy Spirit—who "stooped" to speak and to make a connection to us.

As we consider three aspects to persuasion in part 2, we will need to remember that the Lord, who used words and *the* Word (*Logos*) to connect with those made in His image, draws people to Himself through His Son, who is the Word. He gives us His Word through the Word of God in Scripture, and He connects us to His Word through the Spirit. Persuasion, then, is *God's* way of drawing us to Himself. He does not simply and only *speak* the truth (which He certainly does), but He acts to enter our world, *as one of us*, so that we might be able to enter His world of eternal redemption.

This is the persuasive task of every Christian. We want to discern and initiate a "connection" between us and our audience—"Enter their world," as it were—in order to bring them into the "world" of the gospel and its truth. Thus, we want to choose and use words that have the potential to *connect* to those to whom we speak; we want to avoid words that will repel them.

Maybe an extreme example will help clarify this need for persuasion. Suppose you were to approach an unbeliever, even an unbelieving friend, and say, "By the way, Christianity teaches that if you don't repent and believe in Christ, you will suffer in hell for eternity." There is nothing false about this; Christianity teaches this. You have certainly told your friend the truth, but how persuasive is it?

I remember hearing someone years ago labeling this kind of truth-telling as "the burp effect." Instead of trying to connect and persuade others, we "burp" the truth out. As with a burp, we feel much better, but the other person is offended! Persuasion seeks to avoid the burp effect. It assumes the truth of the gospel but seeks to communicate it with wisdom so that, instead of using words that can easily offend and put off, we try to connect the truth with needs, ideas, and concepts that they already have or accept.

Even as the Lord has connected Himself to us, in and through His Word, and supremely in His incarnation, we hope to learn to employ persuasive words to connect others to the Word Himself. This is a connection that will eternally persist, and it is a connection that, since the entrance of sin, comes in the midst of a war.

TWO

The DIVINE *Defender*

Persuasion is not primarily a technique, if by technique we mean a way of manipulating circumstances in order to get what we want. It runs much deeper than that. To use a biblical word, persuasion is an application of biblical *wisdom*. Biblical wisdom seeks to take biblical truth and communicate it in a way that connects to a particular need, idea, or situation of life. Because our lives are filled with so many different circumstances and contexts, biblical wisdom seeks to discern those contexts and circumstances so that what we say might address the actual situation (Col 4:5).[1]

Neither is persuasion primarily focused on *us*. Given that persuasion's goal is to establish a *connection* between two or more parties, God is the initial persuader. God was the first to connect with something outside of Himself, through His act of creation. Specifically, He speaks *to* and *with* the ones that He has made in His own image. God is the ultimate creator and sustainer of words and their meanings. When He tells Adam and Eve to subdue the earth or not to eat from the forbidden tree, He is perfectly clear in what He says, and Adam and Eve understand Him.

---

1. For a helpful, brief explanation of "Wisdom Literature" in Scripture, see Robert B. Hughes and J. Carl Laney, *Tyndale Concise Bible Commentary*, The Tyndale Reference Library (Wheaton, IL: Tyndale, 2001), 676.

Once they hear God's words, Adam and Eve are responsible to abide by them. So, from the beginning, the One who is infinite, eternal, and unchangeable "stoops down" to speak to His human creatures, and in that way, He initiates fellowship with them in the garden. They are inextricably linked to Him because *He* connects *them* to Himself. They are immediately drawn to Him by His presence and His speech to them. The Lord creates and uses language to persuade.

CRAFTINESS AND CONFLICT

As we know all too well, the connection that God established with Adam and Eve did not remain in its pristine state. When there was no sin, the fellowship between God and those made in His image was unbroken, without blemish or stain. There was clear and untainted communication between the Lord and His human creatures.

It is significant that, on the day when Adam and Eve decided to break the perfect fellowship that God had established with them, the way in which Satan tempted them was to twist *the words* that God had spoken:

> Now the serpent was more crafty than any of the wild animals the Lord God had made. He said to the woman, "*Did God really say,* 'You must not eat from any tree in the garden'?" (Gen 3:1, emphasis mine)

We should pause to ask why Genesis 3 begins the way it does. Why are we told that the serpent was "more crafty" than any of the wild animals the Lord had made? This statement is not meant to be merely descriptive. It is meant, rather, to help us interpret everything else that Satan, via the serpent, has to *say*. It is the craftiness of the serpent, in other words, that motivates him to ask Eve that first question. It is a question about God's *words*.

The first thing this crafty serpent does with Eve is to cause her to reconsider what God had said. He wants Eve to reinterpret God's own words to her and Adam. The serpent, no doubt, knew the prohibition that God had imposed on Adam and Eve in the garden. But he does not come to them and first say, "Eat from the forbidden tree!" There is no "craftiness," no persuasive element, in that approach.

Instead, he wants Eve to consider again the forbidden tree. He wants her to go back to those *words* from God and mull them over in her own mind. So, he plants the seed in Eve's mind that God is a *restricting* God, that He is One who constrains and confines their freedom. He wants Eve to tell him just exactly *how* constraining the Lord is. "Is He so constraining on your freedom," he says in effect, "that you cannot eat from any of these beautiful and marvelous trees?" In this initial part of the temptation, Eve's response to him is appropriate:

> The woman said to the serpent, "We may eat fruit from the trees in the garden, but God did say, 'You must not eat fruit from the tree that is in the middle of the garden, and you must not touch it, or you will die.'"
> (Gen 3:2–3)

Eve's statement, however, comes in the context of the serpent's crafty question, a question that could be less craftily stated this way: "How much has the Lord constrained your freedom?" Given the serpent's question, Eve's sights are now set on God's prohibition; she is forced by the question to consider why God has restricted her at all. "Why this one tree?" she likely begins to think to herself.

Eve's response properly sets the parameters of God's command. She rightly understands that the Lord has provided boundaries for her and Adam in the garden, boundaries that were meant to show Adam and Eve's obedience to the Lord.

They were supposed to subdue the earth, under God's own rule over them. The Lord's dual commands—to subdue the earth *and* not to eat from the forbidden tree—were designed to display God's sovereignty over them. Even as they subdue the earth and have dominion over God's creation, they are also commanded not to eat of the forbidden tree.

Their responsibility to "subdue" and "have dominion" (ESV) over the earth (Gen 1:28), in other words, is a responsibility *under* God; it is a responsibility *within* the boundaries that God has set. It is not a responsibility without limits.

But the crafty serpent wants Eve to see that this rule is *unduly* restrictive. As a matter of fact, he now says to them, if their rule could extend *beyond* God's restrictions, they would, in fact, be more like God Himself:

> "You will not certainly die," the serpent said to the woman. "For God knows that when you eat from it your eyes will be opened, and you will be like God, knowing good and evil." (Gen 3:4–5)

This, for Eve, and Adam who was "with her" (Gen 3:6), was what turned Satan's deception into Adam and Eve's separation from the fellowship they had enjoyed with the Lord. The craftiness of Satan, appealing to their "restricted" life, and convincing them that they would be more "like God," pushed Adam and Eve beyond their God-given boundaries. From that point on, God's creation would never be the same. Instead of an intrinsic *connection* between God and Adam and Eve, shame and brokenness entered in:

> Then the eyes of both of them were opened, and they realized they were naked; so they sewed fig leaves together and made coverings for themselves. Then the man and his wife heard the sound of the LORD God as he was walking in the garden in the cool of the day, and they hid from the LORD God among the trees of the garden. (Gen 3:7–8)

The curse that the Lord now has to bring into creation, and into His fellowship with Adam and Eve, is the beginning of a spiritual war that will continue until the end of time:

> So the LORD God said to the serpent, "Because you have done this, Cursed are you above all livestock and all wild animals! You will

crawl on your belly and you will eat dust all the days of your life. And I will put enmity between you and the woman, and between your offspring and hers; he will crush your head, and you will strike his heel." To the woman he said, "I will make your pains in childbearing very severe; with painful labor you will give birth to children. Your desire will be for your husband, and he will rule over you." To Adam he said, "Because you listened to your wife and ate fruit from the tree about which I commanded you, 'You must not eat from it,' Cursed is the ground because of you; through painful toil you will eat food from it all the days of your life. It will produce thorns and thistles for you, and you will eat the plants of the field. By the sweat of your brow you will eat your food until you return to the ground, since from it you were taken; for dust you are and to dust you will return." (Gen 3:14–19)

This is the most devastating moment in all of history. All devastations after flow from this one. From this point forward, there will be pain and toil for Adam and for Eve. Those things that would have come to them naturally, before their sin, now come with great effort, great agony, and great resistance. From now on, the whole creation will be "subjected to frustration" (Rom 8:20), as creation is now "groaning as in the pains of childbirth" (Rom 8:22).

Most centrally, we see that from this point on, the Lord puts enmity between the offspring of Satan and the offspring of the woman. In other words, because of Adam and Eve's sin, the Lord declares war against Satan and his children.

Note, for example, how Jesus refers back to this event in one of His encounters with the Pharisees:

Jesus said to them, "If God were your Father, you would love me, for I have come here from God. I have not come on my own; God sent me. Why is my language not clear to you? Because you are unable to hear what I say. You belong to your father, the devil, and you want to carry out your father's desires. He was a murderer from the beginning, not holding to the truth, for there is no truth in him. When he lies, he speaks his native language, for he is a liar and the father of lies." (John 8:42–44)

Jesus is reminding His audience that all lies, all murder, all sin, stems from that first lie and murder; it all comes from Satan's success in turning Adam and Eve away from God.

From the moment when Adam and Eve sinned, the "offspring of the serpent" continues the war that began on that day. When they were created, Adam and Eve were given life, and were promised life as long as they did their work and lived their lives within God's own design for His people and His garden. To disobey would bring death. In their disobedience, they chose lies and death over life and truth.

Those who are aligned with the serpent carry out his desires. They show themselves to be his offspring, Jesus says, through their lies and their opposition to life itself. They are, at root, opposed to God Himself. The very *connection* that God had established through His word in the garden was "blocked" and hindered through the false words of the serpent. Those words were used to destroy the connection God had established. Once Adam and Eve believed those words, rather than the Lord's words, they no longer wanted to be connected to the Lord; they hid from Him when they heard Him walking in the garden.

When Jesus refers to Satan as a "murderer from the beginning," He is referring to the discord and destruction that followed Adam and Eve after their sin. Not only did Satan lie to Adam and Eve, but once they determined to follow his words rather than the Lord's, death came to their family (Gen 4:1–17). The entrance of sin into the world brought death to all (Rom 5:12). The Lord is the giver of life; sin brings death to all and seeks to destroy the good gifts that the Lord has given to His creation, and to those made in His image. The connection the Lord initially established is now broken because of sin.

THE DIVINE WARRIOR

There is an extremely important pronouncement in Genesis 3:15 that serves to set the agenda for all of redemptive history:

> And I will put enmity between you and the woman, and between your offspring and hers; he will crush your head, and you will strike his heel.

Because of the disobedience of Adam and Eve, the Lord promises *enmity*. The Hebrew word means "hostility." What was previously peaceful and tranquil has now become hostile. This hostility will be between those who are the offspring of the woman and those who are the offspring of the devil (see, for example, Gen 26:3–5 and John 8:42–44).

It is important to notice that this hostility is put in place *by the Lord Himself*. He says to Adam and Eve, "I will put enmity . . ." Now that sin has entered God's otherwise good creation, the Lord initiates, in effect, a *war* between the offspring of the two "families." As Scripture goes on to teach us, the Lord Himself is committed to fighting that war, even to *leading* the fight of the woman's offspring. He Himself is the Divine Warrior, who fights to defend His holy name.

The Divine Warrior in the Old Testament

It is because of the enmity which was brought about by the sin of Adam and Eve that the reality of, and need for, a defense—an apologetic— comes into play in Scripture. But it is important to recognize that the defense of the Lord against sin in the Old Testament has its primary focus, not in Israel, but in God.

One of the first explicit texts dealing with the Lord confronting and battling His enemies is in the exodus. The children of Israel were slaves in Egypt. The time came for the Lord to set them free from their slavery (see Gen 15:13–14). We see in the opening chapters of Exodus that the Lord chose a mediator, Moses, to bring the people out of Egypt (Exod 3).

However, we also see that it was the Lord Himself who did battle against Pharaoh. For example, in the plagues that were sent to Egypt, we see the Lord sending those plagues in order that Pharaoh would relent and release the people of Israel. Those plagues culminated in the Passover, after which Pharaoh relented and let Israel go:

> All the Israelites did just what the LORD had commanded Moses and Aaron. And on that very day the LORD brought the Israelites out of Egypt by their divisions. The LORD said to Moses, "Consecrate to me every firstborn male. The first offspring of every womb among the Israelites belongs to me, whether human or animal." Then Moses said to the people, "Commemorate this day, the day you came out of Egypt, out of the land of slavery, because *the LORD brought you out of it with a mighty hand.* (Exod 12:50–13:3, emphasis mine)

As the Lord engages the battle against sin, and against those who were His enemies, *He* is the one who is defending His honor, even as He uses Moses (and others) to carry out His plan. It is, centrally, the Lord who is the Divine Warrior. He is the Apologist. The "defense" or apology of the exodus was the Lord's doing, first and foremost.

The word *apology* or *apologetics* is not a word invented by theologians or academics. It is actually a word that the Lord Himself uses in Holy Scripture (for example, in 1 Pet 3:15, the word translated as "give an answer" is the Greek word *apologia*). It is a word that means "to defend," and it assumes the reality of opposition or attack. To "apologize" in this sense does not mean saying you're sorry. It means defending what you believe in the face of questions, or of someone who opposes what you believe, or of someone who might attack your Christian faith. An "apology" is a defense, and it assumes some kind of hostility. In Scripture, it assumes a war.

We see this "defense" as well in the conquest of Canaan. Notice:

> Now when Joshua was near Jericho, he looked up and saw a man standing in front of him with a drawn sword in his hand. Joshua went up

to him and asked, "Are you for us or for our enemies?" "Neither," he replied, "but as commander of the army of the LORD I have now come." Then Joshua fell facedown to the ground in reverence, and asked him, "What message does my Lord have for his servant?" The commander of the LORD's army replied, "Take off your sandals, for the place where you are standing is holy." And Joshua did so. Now the gates of Jericho were securely barred because of the Israelites. No one went out and no one came in. Then the LORD said to Joshua, "See, *I have delivered Jericho* into your hands, along with its king and its fighting men." (Josh 5:13–6:2, emphasis mine)

This passage shows us explicitly who it is that is leading the battle against sin, and against the Lord's enemies. It is the Lord Himself. Joshua sees a warrior in front of him. It is natural for him to ask for whom this warrior plans to fight: "Are you for us or for our enemies?" What Joshua expected was surely not the answer he received. He had asked the wrong question. He hadn't discerned the identity of this warrior.

This warrior was not merely a member of any army. Instead, this was the commander of the Lord's army, and in that sense, He was on neither side. As a matter of fact, this is the Lord of hosts Himself, who has condescended to fight the battle. This is why Joshua was commanded to take off his sandals. Only the presence of the Lord Himself could so sanctify the ground that it was offensive to bring the dirt of the world into it; his sandals must be removed (see also Exod 3:5–6).[2]

As the commander, the Lord makes clear whose battle Joshua is fighting, and whose victory it would be: "See, *I* have delivered Jericho into your hands, along with its king and its fighting men." It is the Lord who

---

2. Though the identity of this Divine Warrior is disputed by some, it seems clear to me that this is the Lord, at least because (1) the command of the Lord for Joshua to take off his sandals *due to the hallowed ground* is identical to that of Exodus 3:5, where the Lord appears to Moses. As with Moses, Joshua falls down in reverence. That reverence would be out of place, at minimum, if this were a creature. And (2), it is clearly said that it is "the Lord" who is speaking and who delivers Joshua from Jericho.

delivered Jericho to Joshua. Joshua was the Lord's instrument to fight the battle, but the battle was the Lord's, and He was the victor.[3]

This pattern of apologetics—defending the Lord's honor against sin—in the Old Testament is that the Lord is the Defender, He is the Warrior, and He often uses others to accomplish His purposes (2 Kgs 19:34; 20:6; Ps 43:1; 72:4; 74:22; Isa 37:35; 38:6). But we should not miss the point that, ever since the entrance of sin, there has been a defense, an apologetic, a confrontation of the Lord in His righteousness against sin and rebellion. The point of this confrontation is so that the nations would know that the Lord alone is God. Justice is exacted and executed by God, specifically to make this clear.

One more Old Testament confrontation in which the Lord fights the battle will set the stage for our move into the New Testament:

> Now the king of Aram was at war with Israel. After conferring with his officers, he said, "I will set up my camp in such and such a place." The man of God sent word to the king of Israel: "Beware of passing that place, because the Arameans are going down there." So the king of Israel checked on the place indicated by the man of God. Time and again Elisha warned the king, so that he was on his guard in such places. This enraged the king of Aram. He summoned his officers and demanded of them, "Tell me! Which of us is on the side of the king of Israel?" "None of us, my lord the king," said one of his officers, "but Elisha, the prophet who is in Israel, tells the king of Israel the very words you speak in your bedroom." "Go, find out where he is," the king ordered, "so I can send men and capture him." The report came back: "He is in Dothan." Then he sent horses and chariots and a strong force there. They went by night and surrounded the city. When the servant of the man of God got up and went out early the next morning, an army with horses and chariots had surrounded the city. "Oh no, my lord!

---

3. For an extensive list of passages in Scripture that refer to the Lord's war against sin and thus to apologetics, see K. Scott Oliphint, *The Battle Belongs to the Lord* (Phillipsburg, NJ: Presbyterian and Reformed Publishing Company, 2003), 195–201.

What shall we do?" the servant asked. "Don't be afraid," the prophet answered. "Those who are with us are more than those who are with them." And Elisha prayed, "Open his eyes, LORD, so that he may see." Then the LORD opened the servant's eyes, and he looked and saw the hills full of horses and chariots of fire all around Elisha. (2 Kgs 6:8–17)

Here we see the Lord fighting, but we see more clearly that the battle the Lord fights is a *spiritual* battle, with spiritual forces arrayed to defeat the Lord's enemies. These forces are every bit as real as the army surrounding Elisha, but their presence can only be seen by those whose eyes are opened by the Lord Himself. Thus, they are spiritually discerned. Clearly the Lord, as the Captain of His army, has arrayed a spiritual army so that His enemies might eventually be subdued and defeated.

The Divine Warrior in the New Testament

The most quoted psalm in the New Testament is Psalm 110.[4] That psalm begins with a command from "the LORD" (Hebrew: *Yahweh*) to "my lord" (Hebrew: *Adonai*):

The LORD says to my lord: "Sit at my right hand until I make your enemies a footstool for your feet." (Ps 110:1)

Here David tells us that the LORD, or *Yahweh*, grants to "my lord," or *Adonai*, the privilege of sitting at His right hand until *Adonai's* enemies are made a footstool for His feet. This is a coronation psalm. It is *Yahweh* recognizing and affirming the cosmic authority of David's lord, *Adonai*. To sit at the right hand of *Yahweh* meant to sit with Him in the place of cosmic authority.

Clearly, this coronation is given to *Adonai* with a view toward warfare. *Adonai* is given a place of authority, with *Yahweh*, so that *His enemies*

---

4. Quoted or referenced in Matt 22:44; 26:64; Mark 12:36; Luke 20:42–43; Acts 2:34–35; 1 Cor 15:25; Eph 1:20–22; Col 3:1; Heb 1:3, 13; 2:8; 5:6; 7:17, 20–21, 24, 28; 8:1; 10:12–13; 12:2; 1 Pet 3:22; Rev 6:17; 19:14, 17–18.

will be subdued. The reign of *Adonai* has a specific purpose in view. It is initiated so that all of His enemies will be conquered. The reign of *Adonai*, with *Yahweh*, is intended to reverse the curse of sin that began in Genesis 3.

But this reign also has an *end* in view. *Adonai* is to sit at *Yahweh's* right hand *until* their enemies are all subdued. That is, He will sit there and reign with *Yahweh* until the warfare is over.

The author to the Hebrews frames much of his discussion around this same psalm. He says:

> The Son is the radiance of God's glory and the exact representation of his being, sustaining all things by his powerful word. After he had provided purification for sins, he sat down at the right hand of the Majesty in heaven. So he became as much superior to the angels as the name he has inherited is superior to theirs. (Heb 1:3–4)

The author has in mind here both the *nature* of the Son, as well as His historic *work*. His nature is nothing short of full deity. As the radiance of God's glory and as the exact representation of God's nature, He is the One who is *from* God and who *is* Himself God. This is why, for example, the author, in verse 6, applies Deuteronomy 32:43 to the Son ("Let all God's angels worship him").[5] As we have seen, the only one who could be worthy of worship in all of Scripture is God Himself. The author to the Hebrews wants to make clear, from the beginning of his epistle, that the Son is God, and is therefore worthy of worship.

But Hebrews also wants us to see that the Son, even as He is always worthy of worship as God, nevertheless "became as much superior to the angels as the name he has inherited is superior to theirs." That is, the author is affirming that it was *the Son* who came to earth to do His work perfectly, and by completing that work He proved that He was, in fact,

---

5. There are some textual technicalities in this verse. For a concise explanation, see Peter T. O'Brien, *The Letter to the Hebrews*, The Pillar New Testament Commentary (Grand Rapids: Eerdmans, 2010), 70–71.

the Son. By virtue of His perfect obedience, He "inherited" the name that was His from all eternity (see also Rom 1:1–4). In other words, the Son, who is fully God, came as the God-*man*, and perfectly obeyed, that He might earn and merit that which was His in the first place.

Once He perfectly performed the work He was given, He "sat down at the right hand of the Majesty in heaven." In other words, what the author is telling us is that it was the person and work of *the Son* that was the fulfillment of Psalm 110. At the completion of His earthly task, He was crowned the King. All authority in heaven and on earth was given to Him (Matt 28:18). He alone was worthy to break the seal and open the scrolls because He was slain, and He purchased for God with His blood men from every tribe and tongue and people and nation (Rev 5:9).

The purpose of the Son's reign, as expressed in Psalm 110, is so that His enemies would be subdued. And there will come a time when every enemy will, in fact, be subdued:

> The last enemy to be destroyed is death. For he "has put everything under his feet." Now when it says that "everything" has been put under him, it is clear that this does not include God himself, who put everything under Christ. When he has done this, then the Son himself will be made subject to him who put everything under him, so that God may be all in all. (1 Cor 15:26–28)

Notice how Paul refers us in this passage to another, similar psalm, Psalm 8:6, in order to affirm the Son's rule and reign. But he also affirms that the Son will reign until the last enemy is destroyed. At that time, the Son (*Adonai*) will hand the kingdom to His Father (*Yahweh*), since the task of subduing His enemies will finally be complete. At that time, God will be "all in all" because sin will be dealt its final death blow, and death will be no more.

In all of this, it is the Divine Warrior, the Son of God Himself, who is reigning and ruling as His enemies are being subdued. The goal of that reign is to squash the rebellion of sin and destruction, which leads to death, and to promote the reality of life and peace over the entire creation. That life and peace, as we see from the New Testament, can only come by way of the Son (see, for example, Luke 1:79; 2:14; 19:38; John 1:4; 3:36; 5:21). Apart from the Son, there is only death.

So the Son, in whom alone is life, is now reigning at the right hand of His Father, as His enemies are in the process of being subdued by Him. He will, eventually, subdue them all, as He fights the cosmic battle against the powers and principalities in the heavenlies (Eph 6:12).

One of the most incredible realities of this war is that the Lord uses His church to fight; He allows us to be engaged in the defense of the faith. Weak and limited vessels of His are the army He has chosen to use in His fight against sin and death.

The Divine Warrior in Our Lives

Christian apologetics recognizes the spiritual war that the Lord Himself initiated when sin entered the world. It is a war that rages in the cosmos. The goal of apologetics is to defend the honor and glory of the Lord, as we fight with and for Him, in the midst of this cosmic war.

Perhaps one of the most familiar "war" passages in the New Testament is Ephesians 6:10–17. This passage helps us see how we are to prepare for the spiritual battle, for the apologetic task of defending the faith. There the apostle Paul describes what it means for us to go "onward" as "Christian soldiers." Notice how he begins this discussion of spiritual warfare:

> Finally, be strong in the Lord and in his mighty power. Put on the full armor of God, so that you can take your stand against the devil's schemes. (Eph 6:10–11)

The strength needed for the battle can only be found "in the Lord and in *His* mighty power." The battle, in other words, is *His* battle; it is a battle that has its focus in the strength and power of the Lord Himself.

In fighting the battle, we are to be fitted with "the whole armor *of*

God." This highlights again that the battle is not, in the first place, *our* battle, but it is God's battle. If we think our armor is meant to be produced by us, we will not stand in battle. Any armor that is man-made is too weak and frail to resist the opposition. As we will see, the armor that we must wear in battle is nothing less than *God's* armor. No other armor has the strength to withstand the schemes of the devil.

What is this armor that God provides for His church? We will have more to say about this as we move along in our discussion of persuasion and apologetics. As many have noted, all of the different elements of God's armor are *defensive*, except one. All of them, except the last one, are meant to *protect us* rather than to be used to *confront* those who would oppose the Lord. The clear indication from the description of this armor is that there will be constant attacks from the enemy. We will need to be sufficiently dressed for this continual and perpetual onslaught.

So, says Paul, we are to, "Stand firm then, with the belt of truth buckled around your waist, with the breastplate of righteousness in place" (Eph 6:14). We see in this verse that Paul is referring us to Isaiah 11:5. This chapter in Isaiah is a prophecy about the coming King. It foretells the righteous reign of the Lord Jesus Christ:

> But with righteousness he will judge the needy, with justice he will give decisions for the poor of the earth. He will strike the earth with the rod of his mouth; with the breath of his lips he will slay the wicked. (Isa 11:4)

Here we are told of this root from the stem of Jesse (v. 1), who is the One who will judge the earth (v. 4). But He will not judge by what His eyes see (v. 3). Instead, He will judge the earth in righteousness (v. 4). Obviously, from this passage, the Messiah-King will be engaged in warfare; He will "strike the earth with the rod of his mouth; with the breath of his lips he will slay the wicked." Just after this affirmation of the King's warfare, Isaiah notes, "Righteousness will be his belt and faithfulness the sash around his waist" (Isa 11:5).

This is the passage that the apostle Paul alludes to in his initial description of our spiritual armor. But there is a significant and substantial difference between Paul's use of this passage, and the passage as Isaiah gives it to us. *In Isaiah, the armor described is not in the first place our armor, but it is the armor worn by the Divine Warrior, the Messiah-King.* It is armor that Christ wears as He carries out His cosmic reign at the right hand of His Father.

Any recipient of Paul's letter to the Ephesians who knew the Old Testament would have readily recognized that the armor that *we* are to put on is the selfsame armor that the Messiah, Christ Himself, put on in order to rule and to reign amid the spiritual battle. Our armor, in other words, is really His armor; it is the armor that we wear *because* He wears it. We fight, only because He does. We defend the faith, only because He is the Divine Apologist.

This serves to bolster our recognition that the battle we fight is, in the first place, *His* battle, not ours. It reminds us that the only reason we have spiritual armor to wear is because our Savior-King first wore it and continues to wear it as He reigns on high. It also reminds us that as we fight the battle—as we engage in Christian apologetics—He is the One who leads the charge, and who accomplishes whatever victories we might experience (see Josh 5:13–15).

The first element of our armor, says Paul, is the "belt of truth" buckled around our waist. We know, from John 17:17, that our offensive piece of armor is the Word of God, which is the truth itself. In that sense, the first and last piece of spiritual weaponry that we put on is *truth*. The truth must bracket all other armor; it surrounds and encompasses the whole outfit.

But the belt of truth must be somehow different from the Word of God, which is truth itself. What might that difference be? We have some clue to the answer to that question when we recognize that Paul is referring us to Isaiah 11:5: "Righteousness will be his belt and faithfulness the sash around his waist." The prophet Isaiah uses a word that is translated "righteousness." This word also carries the idea of that which is just and proper in the world. In other words, the "belt of truth" that is our first piece of armor must include a commitment to righteousness and justice. It is, in that sense, the *application* of what God says in His Word to the way in which we view the world.

What Paul seems to mean by the "belt of truth," then, is that we are to view the world that God has made through the principles of His Word. Righteousness and justice are defined and applied according to biblical principles. This would include, at least, the truth that Christ is now on the throne, reigning in and over the world, even though it may appear to us at times that He is not in control (see Heb 2:8). We don't define justice and righteousness according to worldly principles; we define them according to the Word of God and the reign of Christ as He sits on His Father's throne.

When we understand justice and righteousness in this way, we make significant progress toward a biblical understanding of suffering. Such an understanding is crucial when we are engaged in spiritual warfare. Even when it appears that the wicked prosper and those who follow Christ are being subdued, with the "belt of truth" firmly tied around our waists, we recognize that Christ has already won the victory for His people. Even in our sufferings, therefore, we remain "more than conquerors" (Rom 8:37). Even as we suffer—perhaps *especially* as we suffer—we can defend the Christian faith, engaging in the spiritual war that rages in the heavenlies. We can do this because we know, as those who are outside of Christ cannot know, that "our present sufferings are not worth comparing with the glory that will be revealed in us" (Rom 8:18).

This "belt of truth" is the first and most basic aspect of our spiritual armor. When we put it on for battle, we commit ourselves to viewing the world through the 20/20 lens of biblical truth. This is a radical commitment, and it requires us to filter the flood of data that enters our sensory world every day. It requires us to take all of the arguments, the essays, the opinions, the beliefs, the theories, the constant flow of information all around us, and to scrutinize them according to what the Lord has said in His Word. It requires, in sum, a biblical view of the world.

As with the "belt of truth," the "breastplate of righteousness" is, in the first place, a piece of armor that Yahweh Himself puts on in order to fight the battle against His enemies (Isa 59:17). This righteousness that the Lord puts on demonstrates His opposition to the injustices and the rebellion of those who fight against Him:

Lead me, LORD, in your righteousness because of my enemies—make your way straight before me. (Ps 5:8)

Righteousness, in other words, is a piece of battle armor that stands in bold relief and that brings light against the backdrop of the darkness that surrounds the opposition:

Of the greatness of his government and peace there will be no end. He will reign on David's throne and over his kingdom, establishing and upholding it with justice and righteousness from that time on and forever. The zeal of the LORD Almighty will accomplish this. (Isa 9:7)

So also when we don the Lord's breastplate of righteousness, we fight the battle by exhibiting behavior that conforms to His righteousness. Because there is darkness, we shine the light of the Lord's holiness; because there is injustice, we seek and support the justice that only the Lord Himself can provide; because people commit themselves to false-hoods (see Rom 1:25), we live the truth (1 John 1:6) as we walk according to the Lord's instructions (Gal 5:25). Righteousness and justice are defined according to the light of God's Word, not according to some other human standard.

The next piece of armor that Paul describes is a curious one that has baffled many commentators. What does Paul mean by "your feet fitted with the readiness that comes from the gospel of peace" (Eph 6:15)? What, exactly, is this "readiness" that comes from the gospel of peace?

The most likely explanation is that it is the gospel itself that prepares us for the battle into which we are called. Ironically, it is the gospel of *peace* that prepares us for *battle*. The peace of which Scripture often speaks is the *shalom* of God. We can see this explained succinctly in the so-called "Aaronic benediction" of Numbers 6:24–26:

> "The LORD bless you and keep you; the LORD make his face shine on you and be gracious to you; the LORD turn his face toward you and give you peace."

In this benediction, we have what are called "parallelisms." This means that there is a repetition of meaning in the various clauses and phrases. So, for example, another way to express the phrase "The LORD bless you" is "The LORD make his face shine on you." So also, another way to express the wish that "The LORD be gracious to you" is to say, "The LORD . . . give you peace." Peace, in other words, is a blessing of the Lord, by which He turns His face toward us, by grace, so that the hostility that was between Him and us because of our sin is no longer there. The peace of the Lord, in other words, is His *salvation*, a salvation that comes to us now in and through His gospel of peace. In that gospel, the wall of hostility between a holy God and sinful people is torn down; the barrier is destroyed, and peace between Him and us is given to all who are in Christ.

It is only when we have the belt of truth around our waist and we are wearing the breastplate of righteousness that we understand the cosmic effect of this gospel of peace. The gospel is not simply or only *for us*; it is the gospel whether we affirm it or not. The gospel includes the fact that all authority in heaven and on earth has been given to Christ. Paul reminded his readers of this in Ephesians 1:19–23:

> That power is the same as the mighty strength he exerted when he raised Christ from the dead and seated him at his right hand in the heavenly realms, far above all rule and authority, power and dominion, and every name that is invoked, not only in the present age but also in the one to come. And God placed all things under his feet and

appointed him to be head over everything for the church, which is his body, the fullness of him who fills everything in every way.

The "readiness" of the gospel includes our affirmation and application of the fact that all things have been placed under Christ's feet because He is the head *over everything*. The battle that we fight, in other words, is always and everywhere fought within *His* realm, and on *His* terms, since He rules over it all. Included in His terms is the fact that His gospel is, as Paul puts it, a "gospel of peace."

So we prepare to *fight* for *peace* when we recognize that the One on the throne is subduing His enemies so that there will, in the end, be peace (see Luke 2:14). Just as Jesus is the One who came to preach peace to those who were far off and those who were near (Eph 2:17), so also we prepare ourselves for the same task.

This peace that is the focus of the gospel is rich in biblical meaning. It is the *shalom* of the Old Testament. It is a peace that not only means that wars and battles will cease. More importantly, and more deeply, it means that we, and the world, are reconciled to God. The war that we fight, as we are shod with the readiness of the gospel, is not a war that only brings victory. It is a war that brings peace to all of God's creation. "'The wolf and the lamb will feed together, and the lion will eat straw like the ox, and dust will be the serpent's food. They will neither harm nor destroy on all my holy mountain,' says the Lord" (Isa 65:25). It is the final moment of persuasion, as the apologetic battle comes to an end.

Why would the apostle describe the armor of our "readiness" as footwear? There are, perhaps, a couple of biblical ideas at work here. First, in keeping with the theme of God's rule and reign over all of creation, Isaiah says:

How beautiful on the mountains are the feet of those who bring good news, who proclaim peace, who bring good tidings, who proclaim salvation, who say to Zion, "Your God reigns!" (Isa 52:7)

We will remember that Paul quotes this passage as he argues for the necessity of preachers and of preaching (Rom 10:14–17). The first reason that Paul describes the armor of "readiness" as footwear is because the gospel of peace requires that we *go* in order to communicate it. This aspect of our armor, therefore, highlights the need to go out into the world, into hostile territory, to defend and spread the gospel of peace.

The second biblical idea, which is perhaps at work here, has to do with what footwear sometimes represents in the Old Testament. We will remember, for example, when the Lord appeared to Moses from the burning bush in Exodus 3, the first thing the Lord commanded Moses to do was to remove his sandals (Exod 3:5; see also Josh 5:15). The reason Moses was commanded to remove his sandals was because the presence of the Lord had sanctified the place where He appeared. In other words, Moses was commanded not to bring the dirt of the world into the holy presence of God on that mountain.

When our feet are shod with the readiness of the gospel, the movement is reversed. We move *from* the holy presence of the Lord and *to* the world, in order to engage the battle in the world. To put it in New Testament terms, we respond to, receive and recommit to, the gospel of peace each week in our worship of the Lord within the sanctuary of His people, the church. We then put on our battle boots in order to move from His holy presence in His sanctuary to a hostile and needy world, to fight the good fight. To put it in the language of the Great Commission (Matt 28:19), as we are ready to go from the presence of Christ to the world, we are to take the gospel of peace to all nations in order to make disciples. In that way, it is the gospel of peace that the Lord uses to subdue the world, as He reigns at the right hand of His Father.

Now that we are properly dressed in God's armor, we are told to "take up the shield of faith." We should note here that a shield is not, in the strictest sense, something we wear. It is instead something that is meant to "cover" us in battle. In that sense, as we *take up* the shield of faith, it is our faith that protects us, even as we are dressed in God's armor. The word that Paul uses, which is translated "take up," is the same word he uses in verse 13 when he tells us to "put on" the full armor of God.

The shield that we use in battle, which is the shield of faith, covers and thus characterizes the rest of the armor that we wear. The belt of truth, the breastplate of righteousness, the shoes of readiness, all of these are what they are because they have as their focus our trust in Christ. We see the world through the lenses of Scripture because we trust that what we have in our Bibles is the very Word of God. We conform our character to biblical principles of justice and righteousness because we trust that God's ways and Christ's own character are alone truly righteous and just. We put on our battle boots of readiness because we trust that the reign of Christ will actually bring about the subduing of His enemies by way of the gospel of peace. Scripture guarantees us that Christ's enemies will, one day, be entirely subdued (Phil 2:10–11).

In other words, the entirety of our armor is meant to be bathed in the shield of faith. It is our trust in Christ that gives our armor its ability to protect us. Without that trust, we have no truth, there is no righteousness, and we cannot be prepared by and for the gospel of peace.

For example, we have been at pains to highlight the fact that Jesus Christ now rules and reigns at the right hand of the Father. However, "at present we do not see everything subject to them" (Heb 2:8). In order to set firmly in our minds the fact that Christ now reigns, therefore, we need the shield of faith. We trust what God has said.

We see the world, not initially with our physical eyes, but with the eyes of faith as we prepare to engage the apologetic battle. If we divert our attention, if we let down our guard and lay down our shield, then we are ill-equipped to fight the battle. If our shield is down, then our belt of truth is too weak to support us, our breastplate of righteousness is thin and penetrable, and our boots of readiness falter.

This shield of faith, we should note, is able to "extinguish all the flaming arrows of the evil one." This reminds us again that "our struggle is not against flesh and blood, but against the rulers, against the authorities, against the powers of this dark world and against the spiritual forces of evil in the heavenly realms" (Eph 6:12). Even though we engage the battle with other people who oppose our Savior and His reign, we should recognize that the battle rages in the realm of the invisible. It is that realm that supports and encourages the opposition that we face.

Notice that our shield of faith does not simply *stop* the flaming arrows that are fired at us. It is a more effective shield than that. The shield of faith is able to *extinguish* those arrows. It is, as it were, doused in the living water of the gospel so that when the flames hit, they are not only stopped, but they are immediately quenched. The shield destroys the power and ability of the flames to destroy. Instead of the flames spreading, they are snuffed out when we are armed with trust in our heavenly Father and in His Word.

The language that points us to the final two pieces of armor is significant. The command in verse 17 is to "take" the helmet of salvation and the sword of the Spirit. Other pieces of armor are to be put on, but here the emphasis is on that which we have *received.*

Paul has already emphasized to the Ephesians that the salvation that we have by grace is a salvation that is a *gift* (Eph 2:1–10). There is nothing we can *do* that will accomplish our salvation. If we are to be saved, *God* must save us.

This is good news in our fight against the Lord's enemies. At some point, the Lord subdued us with the good news of His gospel. And because *He* is the One that subdued us, He will never let us go (see John 10:29; Rom 8:38–39). Our salvation begins and ends with the Lord's work. First, He works in history. His death and resurrection were designed to take away God's wrath and to satisfy His justice. Then, He works in us, changing our hearts of stone to hearts of flesh (Ezek 36:26), and uniting us to His Son.

We engage in persuasive apologetics as those who are servants of the King, and who dwell in His kingdom. We serve Him and dwell there because He has given us entrance and has called us His own.

This is the helmet of salvation. As with the other pieces of armor, it is, in the first place, a piece that the Lord Himself has worn (see Isa 59:17).

The Lord's helmet of salvation is one wherein He conquers His enemies. He subdues them by His own power and work.

For us, on the other hand, it is His helmet, and it testifies that He is the One who can subdue His enemies and who alone has the power to accomplish the salvation that is needed. Defense and persuasion are, in the first place, His activities in the spiritual battle.

This helmet of salvation is a piece of armor that has its focus on the head. In Paul's description, it is a helmet *of salvation*. In that sense, it sums up the entire reality of the gospel in our lives. It includes, for example, what we *know*. We know that we are His. We know that we are His because of what He has done in history and in us. And we know that, even in our defense of the faith, the faith that we defend is not ours by right, but is ours by grace. We have received it because He has been gracious to grant it to us. Anyone else who would receive it would and could only do so by His grace.

This should give us confidence in our apologetic. It should embolden us in the fight. We stand where we are, and we are who we are, not because of anything in us, but solely because of Him. As we battle against unbelief, we do so in full recognition that we are recipients of His grace, and that such grace is undeserved.

This keeps us from an arrogant and judgmental spirit in our spiritual fight. It ensures that we fight, not as those who are intrinsically able and equipped, but as those who have received a great gift, and who long for others to receive it as well. The helmet of salvation is an echo of Paul's confidence:

> That is why I am suffering as I am. Yet this is no cause for shame, *because I know whom I have believed*, and am convinced that he is able to guard what I have entrusted to him until that day. (2 Tim 1:12)

The last piece of armor, another piece which we are to "take" and receive is the "sword of the Spirit, which is the word of God." This, as we mentioned above, is the only offensive piece of armor that we have.

In that sense, it is different from all the rest. This piece is so important, especially in the context of apologetics and persuasion, that we will need to give it a particular focus in the next chapter.

THE LORD'S BATTLE

As soon as Adam and Eve brought sin into the world, the Lord determined to subdue and conquer it (Gen 3:15). He could have destroyed it and all its effects immediately. There is nothing about the presence of sin that *requires* the Lord to battle it throughout history. But He determined that history would be defined, in part, by this ongoing battle. The outcome of the battle has never been in doubt. In this particular battle, the two sides are not equal. As with all things in creation, the Lord sovereignly controls all that comes to pass.

The reason the battle rages is so that the Lord Himself would be glorified in and through the battle (Rom 11:36). He continues to fight the battle so that we, His creatures, might continually see His character and His glory against the backdrop of the ugly and destructive nature of sin (Rom 8:18–19).

It is the Lord who is the Great Apologist. He defends His character against the tenacious and insidious attacks of those who would oppose Him, both here on earth and in the heavenlies. He is, throughout redemptive history, the Divine Warrior.

In this battle, He chooses weak, frail, finite, and sinful creatures like us to be involved. The armor that He Himself wears in the battle is now the armor that we are to wear as we seek, persuasively, to defend the Christian faith.

Every battle requires preparation, and preparation must be thoughtful and intentional. To rush foolishly into battle is to ensure defeat. The Lord gives us specific instructions in His Word about how we can best prepare for the battle to which He has called us.

As we have seen, the preparation required is that we don the proper armor. And the proper armor, as we have also recognized, is the very armor that the Lord Himself has worn for battle.

We see in redemptive history that the Lord fights the battle against His enemies, and He fights that battle using us as His soldiers. As we engage in that battle—which is what apologetics is—responding to objections, challenging others in their unbelief, our focus must always be on the One who is "commander of the army of the LORD" (Josh 5:14). We are given the privilege of fighting with our captain. We battle against heavenly powers. In all of this, however, the captain has assured us of the final outcome.

It is not up to us, therefore, to *win* the battle; the Lord Himself has already done that. It is up to us to prepare ourselves for the battle, and to engage it, so that it will become obvious, more and more, whose battle it is and what the final outcome will be.

As we put on and receive the full armor of God, we ready ourselves for the war that continues until Christ returns and finally subdues all of His enemies, even death (1 Cor 15:26).

It is instructive to notice how Paul concludes his exhortation that we properly prepare for battle: "And pray in the Spirit on all occasions with all kinds of prayers and requests. With this in mind, be alert and always keep on praying for all the Lord's people" (Eph 6:18). Surely Paul concludes his message this way in order to remind us of two key aspects to this battle: First, it is a spiritual battle, and spiritual battles require spiritual weapons. Second, the weapons themselves are not sufficient. As we prepare, we are to "pray in the Spirit" and to "be alert."

The command to pray sets our focus in the proper direction. It causes us to fix our gaze, not on the horizontal activity that is right in front of our eyes, but on the vertical relationship we have with the One who is fighting as our Captain. Without such a focus, we could be tempted to misconstrue the battle and its final goal.

As we pray, we are also exhorted to be alert. The idea here is that we are always to be on guard. Since we have put on the full armor of God, it is our responsibility to be alert to the challenges and objections that come at us from various sides. It would do us no good to be fully armored, but asleep. Because we are fully armored, we look to our captain in prayer, and we keep our eyes open so that the Lord's enemies will gain no foothold in the battle.

It should be a great comfort for us to know that the battle to which the Lord calls us is *His* battle in the first place. And because it is His battle, He is the One, in the end, who fights it. He fights the battle with His own armor, as we have seen. But as He calls us to the privilege of fighting with Him, He gives us the very armor that He Himself wears. He does that because it is His armor alone that is adequate for the fight. We cannot arm ourselves with anything that would be sufficient for the battle. As we arm ourselves with His armor, we acknowledge that the battle belongs to the Lord.

A number of years ago, I was invited to a local university to debate the problem of evil with one of their philosophy professors. It was actually more of a discussion than a debate, as I presented my own view and then he presented his, with a question-and-answer time after our presentations.

There are various ways to discuss the problem of evil, but I decided it was best for the audience to recognize, in the end, that whatever questions might remain about that problem, the Lord Himself had come down to *suffer* and to *die* in order to destroy the evil that seeks to oppose Him. In other words, the Lord "connected" Himself to that very problem by immersing Himself in it, as well as its effects (2 Cor 5:21; Heb 2:14–18). As I thought about what I should say at that university, I was conscious of the fact that I was going into battle and that I needed all of the battle resources the Lord gives in order to engage it.

At the end of the question-and-answer time, one student stood up, and with some emotion, pointed his finger at me and the philosophy professor and said something like, "I want each of you to tell me this: Why should I believe anything you have said tonight?" This question was a challenge to both speakers. It was a challenge of persuasion and of our authority. What about each of us, he was asking, would move him to believe what we had said. How might you answer a question like that?

If you were defending and commending the gospel, what would your response be to that question?

Because I had heard questions similar to this from my own students, I recognized the important point behind the question. What the student was, in fact, asking for was a connection between himself and what we had said. His question went to the heart of the "debate."

The philosophy professor motioned to me to go to the microphone first. I went up to the mic and decided that since the student had challenged me, I would challenge him in turn. So, since lecture and questions were over, I said something like this: "You have asked a good question. Why *should* you believe me? Let me respond with my own challenge. The answer to your question is, you shouldn't believe me. But here is what I would challenge you to do. When you leave here, go back to your dorm room, find a Bible somewhere, and open it to the Gospel of John. Read that Gospel from the first to the last. And here is what you need to understand: If you accept my challenge and you read the Gospel of John, you are duty-bound, under God, to believe what it says."

Can you see the point? Can you see how I tried to connect his challenge to my own presentation? He was rightly concerned with the authority of the speakers. He wanted to know if there was something in us that would place an onus on him to believe one of us. I could have talked to him about my own teaching experience, publications, and academic research (which is what the philosophy professor did after me). But none of that would have been sufficient for the Lord's battle. The Lord's battle requires the Lord's own authority, so I connected his concern to my commitment to the persuasive authority of Scripture. If the battle that day was simply mine to fight, I would not have answered as I did. Since it is the Lord's battle, it was my delight to refer this student to what Christ Himself says. In that way, the Lord's own armor, which was mine in the battle, helped me to see the battle for what it really was, and, by God's grace, to place the persuasive authority for my discussion in its proper place, the Holy Spirit speaking by and with the Word of God.

The sword of the Spirit, which is the Word of God, is God's chosen offensive weapon for us. With it, we strike at the heart of Christ's enemies. With it, the Holy Spirit is able persuasively to penetrate to the depth of sin's destruction.

We need now to look more closely at this weapon, in order to recognize the power it possesses in the battle. It is this Word, the very speech of God, that allows for an apologetic that is persuasive, as well as for persuasion that properly defends the Christian faith.

THREE

The DIVINE *Sword*

After class one day, a student approached me to tell me about a recent experience he had at a conference on apologetics. He told me that when the first speaker at the conference began his lecture, he said this: "Last year, our conference focused on the sovereignty of God. Because of that focus, when I began to speak, I said to you all, 'Open your Bibles.' This year, our topic is apologetics, so you will not need to open your Bibles." The student was understandably perplexed by this.

Why do you think a speaker at a conference on Christian apologetics might begin this way? What would lead such a speaker to believe that apologetics is something other than a biblical discipline?

The sword of the Spirit is the only part of our Christian armor meant for offense as we prepare for the Lord's battle. Every other part of our armor shields us and protects us from sin and its effects. But the sword of the Spirit is meant for "striking" the Lord's enemies. We strike them with the very truth of God as it is found in His Word. We learn from Ephesians 6:17 that the sword is both "of the Spirit" and is "the word of God." What is Paul referring to in these two phrases?

In order to set this out clearly, we will need to dive fairly deeply. The ways in which Scripture gives us a proper view of the Word of God and its relation to the Spirit of God are wonderfully rich and multifaceted. What we hope to do below is weave together this colorful biblical tapestry. As we move forward, the biblical notion of the Word and Spirit in the art of persuasion will be ever before us. Our concentration on these glorious truths will repay rich dividends for us as we consider our place in the Lord's battle.

THE WORD AND THE SPIRIT

As we might expect, since Paul appears to be following the themes of Isaiah 11 as he sets out our spiritual armor in Ephesians 6, there is a particular emphasis on the power of the Word to subdue the Messiah's enemies. In Isaiah 11:4, the prophet says:

> He will strike the earth with the rod of his mouth; with the breath of
> his lips he will slay the wicked.

In this verse, we see what is sometimes called a "hendiadys." A hendiadys is present when one thing is explained in two different ways; the word itself means explaining one (Greek: *hen*) by two (Greek: *duoin*). So, what Isaiah says in the first clause is the same thing he says, but in a different way, in the second clause. To "strike the earth with the rod of his mouth" is the same as "with the breath of his lips he will slay the wicked." To put it more generally, the weapon that the Messiah will use is a rod, which is the breath of His lips.

In Scripture, the words used for Spirit in both the Old Testament and the New are the same words used for wind or breath. Context determines how they are best translated, but oftentimes they are meant to refer to the Spirit Himself. So it is in this passage. What Isaiah is saying in this verse is that the Messiah will come in judgment and will judge the earth with the rod of the Spirit, which is the breath of His lips.

This same idea is found in Paul's second letter to the Thessalonians:

> For the secret power of lawlessness is already at work; but the one who
> now holds it back will continue to do so till he is taken out of the way.

And then the lawless one will be revealed, whom the Lord Jesus will
overthrow with the breath of his mouth and destroy by the splendor of
his coming. (2 Thess 2:7–8)

The Lord Jesus will overthrow the lawless one "with the breath of
his mouth." This clause could just as well have been translated "with the
Spirit of his mouth." As we saw in Isaiah, so also here; it is the Spirit,
as the breath of the Messiah, who is instrumental in the battle against
His enemies. The Spirit proceeds from the mouth of the Messiah, who
Himself is the eternal Word.

In that central passage on the nature of Scripture, Paul has both of
these aspects in view:

All Scripture is God-breathed and is useful for teaching, rebuk-
ing, correcting and training in righteousness, so that the servant of God may be thoroughly equipped for every good work.
(2 Tim 3.16–17)

The word that is translated "God-breathed" is the Greek word
theopneustos. It could be translated "God-Spirited." It means that all
Scripture is "from the mouth of God," breathed out, or we could say
"Spirited out," to us by God Himself. The point Paul is making is that
there is an unbreakable and intimate connection between the Spirit of
God and the Word of God.

These two crucial and foundational aspects of our spiritual battle,
of its defense (apologetics) and of our attempts at persuasion, are like
two sides of the same coin, and we need to recognize that they are
inextricably linked. They are the Word and the Spirit. Without these
two, or without their necessary link, our defense and the possibility
of persuasion is in vain. Everything that we think about the relationship of apologetics to persuasion must have these two aspects centrally in view—"The sword of the Spirit, which is the word of God"
(Eph 6:17).

THE WILDERNESS

It will help us at this point to recognize how Jesus Himself viewed these two necessary aspects of our persuasive defense. We see them displayed, for example, in His temptation in the wilderness. Just after Jesus is baptized, inaugurating His messianic ministry, the same Spirit who descended on Him at His baptism leads Him into the wilderness to be tempted:

> Then Jesus was led by the Spirit into the wilderness to be tempted by the devil. After fasting forty days and forty nights, he was hungry. The tempter came to him and said, "If you are the Son of God, tell these stones to become bread." Jesus answered, "It is written: 'Man shall not live on bread alone, but on every word that comes from the mouth of God.'" (Matt 4:1–4)

Jesus's ministry begins where Adam's innocence ended—with the devil's temptation. No doubt the devil thought his success in the garden could easily be repeated in the wilderness. He had brought ruin to the first Adam. His mission was to do the same to the second Adam.

As it was in the garden, so it was in the wilderness; the devil begins his temptation with food. Surely, if he had succeeded in making Adam eat from the forbidden tree, even in the midst of an abundance of food, it should be no problem to make Jesus provide His own food in the midst of His severe hunger.

In both cases, with Adam in the garden and now with Jesus in the wilderness, the devil's temptation could be characterized this way: "You need to eat what God has not given you." In other words, you need to act for yourself, since your Father won't act for you; since He doesn't care, you must care for yourself." (This, in one sense, is the focus of all sins—a lack of trust in what our Father is doing for us.)

Jesus knew that He was being tempted. And He knew that His hunger in the wilderness was being used as a focus of this first temptation.

Adam and Eve's temptation was not based on this kind of need; they were given all that they needed in the garden.

But the devil thought he could use the same approach with Jesus. He's saying something like this: "Whatever the circumstances the Lord has put you in, whether the abundance of the garden or the desolation of the wilderness, your Father has not adequately provided for you. He won't let you eat what you obviously need." That was his ploy in the garden, and he tries it again with Jesus in the wilderness.

All things being equal, there would have been nothing wrong with Jesus turning the stones into bread. Jesus actually did miraculously provide needed food under other circumstances (see, for example, Matt 14:15–21). But all things were not equal. The devil was trying to convince Jesus that His Father was not meeting His needs. He was trying to urge Him to take matters into His own hands. Surely, there would be nothing wrong with using His divine power as the Son of God to feed Himself, would there?

There would. It would have shown that Jesus did not trust what His Father had told Him. This is why Jesus's response to the devil is so magnificently instructive to us. Jesus is not simply using a verse of Scripture to renounce the devil's temptation. He is doing much more than that.

He is saying to the devil in this first temptation that His messianic mission, His reason for living, is to do what His Father has told Him to do. "You simply do not understand," Jesus, in effect, says to the devil, "that my life is motivated *solely* by every single word that my Father has uttered. You foolishly think that I delight in food, but I delight to do the will of my Father" (cf. Gen 3:6; Ps 40:7–8; and Heb 10:7).

Adam and Eve should have said the same thing. They should have told the devil that their lives were motivated by what God had said to them, and not by what food was available or not available to them. Adam and Eve failed because they believed that what God had *forbidden* them was more central to their continued existence than what God had *said* to them. Jesus recognizes that His own ministry is defined, not by what He eats, or even *if* He eats, but by "every word that proceeds out of the mouth of God" (Matt 4:4 NASB).

We see here that in this titanic apologetic struggle—the quintessential spiritual battle—between the Son of God and the father of lies, Jesus makes clear that He is who He is and does what He does according to "every word" that His Father has spoken. In other words, the devil's temptation is thwarted because Jesus recognizes, as Adam and Eve did not, that His circumstances are to be understood in light of what God has said, and not in light of some pretended lack of provision.

The passage Jesus uses in this temptation is taken from Deuteronomy 8:3. In Deuteronomy, Moses is reminding the children of Israel that when they were in the wilderness, the Lord was testing them "to know what was in your heart" (8:2). In the wilderness, He provided manna for them. He gave them what they needed, and in this provision for them He was teaching them that they were to live by every word that proceeds from the mouth of God.

In other words, part of their testing included the fact that it was not the *manna* that was to be seen as their most basic need; the purpose of the manna was to point them to that which *was* their most basic need. What they needed in the wilderness, Moses is saying to them, was every word that proceeded from the mouth of the Lord Himself. The children of Israel should have understood the Lord's provision in that way.

Like Israel of old, Jesus is being tested in the wilderness as well. His test, like Israel's, sets the need for food over against the need for the Word of God. Jesus's response to the devil about His need for food reveals to us His view of Scripture. The devil's temptation assumes the Father had not provided for Jesus, so that He must perform a miracle in order to provide for Himself. Jesus's response rebukes the devil's assumption and focuses the reality of the Father's provision, not on temporal and earthly food, but on the lasting food of God's Word.

For Jesus, the Old Testament is not simply various texts written by various men over a long period of time. Instead, Jesus viewed His Bible as "every word that proceeds from the mouth of God." Every word of the Old Testament is, itself, God-*breathed*. It is both Word and Spirit; the Word of God is the very breath (Spirit) of God.

When Paul tells us that all Scripture is "God-breathed," he is uniting the Word with the Spirit in the same way. "Every word that proceeds from the mouth of God" is every word that God has breathed, or "Spirited" out. Or, as Peter puts it, "For no prophecy was ever produced by the will of man, but *men spoke* from God as they were carried along *by the Holy Spirit*" (2 Pet 1:21 ESV, emphasis mine). Those who were commissioned by the Lord to communicate His Word did not do so according to what *they* wanted to say. Instead, these men spoke from God because the Spirit "carried them along." In their prophecy, in other words, these men were mostly passive; the Spirit carried them so that they would communicate what *He*, not they, wanted them to say. What they spoke was every Spirit-wrought word that proceeds from the very mouth of God. This is how Jesus Himself viewed God's Word. The prophets of old and the apostles who were called to write down that Word wrote, not their own ideas, but the very words of God.

THE UPPER ROOM

The temptation in the wilderness happened at the beginning of Jesus's ministry. As His ministry on earth was drawing to a close, Jesus gathered His disciples together in an upper room in order to prepare them for His departure. As He prepares them, He wants them to better understand who God is as Father, Son, and Holy Spirit. Part of what Jesus wants His disciples to understand about the Trinity is how the three work together to give the Word of God, through the Spirit of God, to the church of God.

It would be encouraging and instructive to read through the entire Upper Room Discourse in John 13–17 with this in mind. In the meantime, however, we can select some key passages that illustrate how Jesus tied together the ministry of the Spirit with the communication of His Word to us. (It might be helpful to you if you have your Bible with you as you read through this section.)

As we read through the Upper Room Discourse, we need to remember that much of what Jesus is communicating to His disciples in the upper room is meant for *them*, first of all, and is not meant to be applied to the rest of us in the same way. In other words, we should read this discourse in the upper room as the transcript of a "private meeting" as the Head of the church gathers His key leaders together behind closed doors in order to make provision for His people in the future, in light of His impending departure.

In this "private meeting," and just after Jesus washes His disciples' feet, He tells them this: "Very truly I tell you, whoever accepts anyone I send accepts me; and whoever accepts me accepts the one who sent me" (John 13:20). In this one statement, Jesus has ensured His disciples that His own authority, in and through His Word, will not leave when He leaves. Instead, He tells them that, even as He Himself is the One who has been sent by His Father (see John 12:49), so also, when He departs from this earth, His disciples will be the ones who have been sent by Him, and anyone who receives them will be receiving Him. Clearly, His earthly and bodily departure does not mean His authority and presence will immediately go as well. It means that His authority is now located in those whom He has chosen to carry on His ministry. But how could this be?

It could be, because of the Holy Spirit:

All this I have spoken while still with you. But the Advocate, the Holy Spirit, whom the Father will send in my name, will teach you all things and will remind you of everything I have said to you. (John 14:25–26)

A time is coming, says Jesus to His disciples, after I depart, when the Holy Spirit will be sent by the Father in Christ's name. When He comes, He will both teach you and remind you. He will teach you and remind you, says Jesus, of "everything *I have said* to you."

In other words, just as the Holy Spirit has been the one "breathing out" the Word of God from the beginning, so also, after Jesus departs, the Spirit will come in a special way and He will continue to "breathe out" the words which Jesus has spoken. The Spirit will teach and remind the disciples of "every word that proceeds" from their Savior.

Then, a bit later, Jesus elaborates on this truth, and says to His disciples:

> "When the Advocate comes, whom I will send to you from the Father —the Spirit of truth who goes out from the Father—he will testify about me. And you also must testify, for you have been with me from the beginning." (John 15:26–27)

So, as Jesus prepares His disciples for His departure, the progression will be this: the Spirit will come and testify about Christ, and then His disciples "also must testify." Jesus will leave and go to His Father, the Father will then send the Holy Spirit in the name of Jesus. The Spirit will "go out from the Father," and His mission will be to testify about Christ.

Here we see that the Spirit will be sent so that what He says, the disciples will say. It is the Spirit and the Word—"The sword of the Spirit, which is the word of God"—continuing *after* Jesus departs.

There are a couple of key and central points that Jesus is making here that need to be highlighted for us as we think about the link between the Word and the Spirit in our persuasive efforts. First, Jesus calls the Spirit the "Spirit of truth." This designation is given to the Spirit just after Jesus told His disciples that *He* is the truth (John 14:6).

It is for this reason that Jesus goes on to say that the Spirit "will testify about me." In other words, since He is the Spirit of truth, and since Jesus is the truth, the Spirit will come to testify about Jesus. (This is one reason why the Spirit is designated "the Spirit of Christ." See Rom 8:9).

Jesus reiterated this truth a little later in this same upper room when He told His disciples that the Spirit's ministry would be to glorify Jesus. Notice the similarities with the previous passage:

"I have much more to say to you, more than you can now bear. But when he, the Spirit of truth, comes, he will guide you into all the truth. He will not speak on his own; he will speak only what he hears, and he will tell you what is yet to come. He will glorify me because it is from me that he will receive what he will make known to you." (John 16:12–14)

Even after He departs, Jesus tells His disciples that He will "have much more to say" to them. The clear emphasis in the passage is on the words of Christ. This is why Jesus again identifies the Spirit as the "Spirit of truth."

And, once again, since He is the Spirit *of truth*, He will glorify the one who is the truth. He will do that by guiding the disciples into "all truth." And He will guide them into all truth by speaking what He hears, that is, by taking from what belongs to Jesus and making it known to them. Here we have the continuation of the Word by and through the Spirit, who will be sent when Jesus departs.

This is, no doubt, another reason why the apostle John identifies Christ as "the Word" at the beginning of his Gospel. He is the Word because He Himself is the one through whom the Father has spoken (Heb 1:1–2). The Father spoke His Word "in the beginning" and will continue to speak His Word, through His Son, by the Spirit, when the Son goes to be with His Father.

In that sense, the Spirit of the Word will come from the Father and the Word, and will make the Word known to *His disciples*, so that they can make that Word known to *us*. The Spirit's ministry is a ministry of the Word, which is the Word of Christ. The sword of the Spirit is the Word of God.

As we mentioned above, Jesus's discourse in this upper room to His disciples highlights in a unique way the Trinitarian character and work of God. It teaches them that His departure will usher in a new era for the Spirit (see John 7:39).

That era will be "new" because the Spirit's ministry will now be defined according to the *completed* work of the Son, the Word, the one who alone is the truth. In other words, the inextricable link between the Word and the Spirit that has been present from the beginning will soon reach its climax in the completed work of the Son, and in the sending of the Spirit to the disciples.

But there is a second central aspect to this symbiosis of the Word and the Spirit that Jesus highlights in John 15:26–27 above. It is an aspect that is more subtle, and is in its subtlety, more magnificently Trinitarian in its depth and majesty.

Jesus is focused in the upper room on teaching His disciples about the Trinity, and about the ways in which each of the three persons accomplish their respective tasks in the world. As the church through the centuries has sought faithfully and biblically to articulate the central identity of each of the persons of the Trinity, it has done so by using a word unique to each of the three, which also describes the relationship of each to the other two.

Because Scripture speaks of the Son as *begotten* of the Father, it is typical to describe the Father as the one who begets the Son, but is Himself *unbegotten*. And since the Son is the *only* begotten of the Father, the Holy Spirit cannot be described in the same way that the Son is.

For centuries, the church has confessed that the Father is *unbegotten*, the Son is *begotten*, and the Holy Spirit is the one who *proceeds* from the Father and the Son.[1] There is an abundance of rich biblical and theological background to these important words that is well worth pursuing.

The point we want to grasp here is that this notion of the Holy Spirit *proceeding* overlaps beautifully with Jesus's words in John 15 above. When

---

1. For example, the "Constantinopolitan Creed" of 381 AD, says, "We believe in one God, the Father Almighty, Maker of heaven and earth, and of all things visible and invisible. . . . And in one Lord Jesus Christ, *the only begotten Son of God, begotten of the Father before all worlds* (æons) . . . And in the Holy Ghost, the Lord and Giver of life, *who proceedeth from the Father,* who with the Father and the Son together is worshiped and glorified, who spake by the prophets." Philip Schaff, *The Creeds of Christendom, with a History and Critical Notes: The History of Creeds*, vol. 1 (New York: Harper & Brothers, Publishers, 1878), 29, my emphases.

Jesus says to His disciples that the "Spirit of truth" is the one "who *goes out* from the Father," the word translated "goes out" can also be translated "proceeds." As a matter of fact, when Jesus tells Satan that man lives by every word that *proceeds* from the mouth of God, the same word is used there as is used in John 15. Every word *proceeds* from the mouth of God, even as the Spirit *proceeds* from the Father.

Whenever theologians make distinctions among the three persons of the Trinity—each of whom is the One God—they distinguish the Father as the One who *begets* and who is *unbegotten*, the Son is the One *begotten*, and the Spirit is the One who *proceeds* from the Father and the Son. In this sense, there is an inextricable link between that which *proceeds* and the Spirit Himself, as the third person of the Trinity.

The point, again, is that this "mystical union" (as we might call it) between the Word and the Spirit is a deep and rich biblical truth to which Jesus Himself gives testimony as He prepares His disciples for His ascension and for their apostolic tasks. To refer again to Jesus's own language, "every word that *proceeds* from the mouth of God" is equivalent to Paul's use of the *theopneustos* character of Holy Scripture; every word is "God-Spirited." The word of the Old and New Testament *proceeds*, even as the Spirit *proceeds*. And Jesus is telling His disciples that the Spirit who will soon proceed from the Father, will do so in order to glorify the one who is the Word Himself, Jesus Christ. And when the Spirit proceeds from the Father, He will tell the disciples the "much more" that Jesus had to say to them.

Finally, as the Upper Room Discourse draws to a close, John records for us Jesus's prayer to His "Holy Father" (John 17:11). It is a prayer that contains a lifetime of biblical truth, as Jesus considers His own ministry, in relation to the Father, the Spirit, His disciples, the world, and the church. Surely a richer, deeper, and more majestic prayer has never been uttered.

As Jesus recognizes that His hour has finally come, His first petition to His Father is this, "Glorify your Son, that your Son may glorify you" (John 17:1). Most commentators will rightly point out that Jesus is asking

His Father to display His Son's life and ministry in all its incomprehensible wisdom, as it culminates in the crucifixion and resurrection of the Son. In other words, Jesus is asking the Father to show the world the Father's wisdom in the Son.

We have already seen how Jesus has just spoken to His disciples of the Spirit's ministry in relation to the Son's own glory. Jesus told His disciples that when the "Spirit of truth" comes, "He will not speak on his own; He will speak only what He hears, and He will tell you what is yet to come. *He will bring glory to me* by taking from what is mine and making it known to you . . ."

Given all that Jesus has said to prepare His disciples for His departure, we should see that when Christ offers this first request to the Father, "Glorify your Son," He is, in fact, *praying to the Father to send the Spirit.* He is, in effect, praying that the One who will "bring glory" to him, whom He has already said is the "Spirit of truth," will be sent to carry on Christ's work on earth.

This is why this first part of Christ's prayer in John 17:1–5 is so "earthly" focused. For example, notice that Christ affirms that the Father granted him authority over all so that He might give eternal life to all the Father had given Him (v. 2). This granting of authority from the Father reaches its apex after Christ's work on earth is done (Matt 28:18), even as the granting of eternal life *to all* the Father had given Him must have its focus in Christ's future ministry on earth, through the Spirit. Only in the future, as history moves on, will *all* that the Father had given Him be given eternal life.

In other words, as Christ offers this first prayer request to His Father, this request and the following four verses have their focus beyond the cross and resurrection, in Christ's completed work, and the ministry that will ensue upon its completion. That ministry will be the inauguration of the Spirit's new ministry (see John 7:39), beginning at Pentecost. The Father will glorify the Son when, with the Son in His presence, He sends the Spirit for that very purpose.

Then Jesus says that He has brought the Father glory by finishing the work the Father gave Him to do. At the time of the prayer, that work was not yet finished. But Jesus is looking past that work, to its completion. As He begins this prayer, His focus is on His work as completed, since "the hour has come." Then, in John 17:5, Jesus prays once again that the Father would glorify Him: "And now, Father, glorify me in your presence with the glory I had with you before the world began." As Jesus looks toward the future, He sees the time, soon to come, when He will again be in the presence of His Father. His prayer is that the Father would glorify Him *in the Father's presence.* This might sound, initially, like the glory itself is meant to be a glory that is located in, and brought about by, the Father's presence.

The request in verse 5 is virtually the same as the request in verse 1. These two requests "bracket" the verses in between and help us interpret them. As with the first request of Jesus, so also with this one. His prayer that the Father would glorify Him in the Father's presence is, in part, a prayer that once Jesus is in the Father's presence, the Spirit would be sent to glorify the Son.

Jesus had just told His disciples that He was going to the Father, and that when He goes, the Spirit of truth would come (John 16:10, 13). One of the reasons the Spirit of truth will come is because Jesus has "much more *to say*" (16:12). And, as we have seen, when the Spirit comes, His mission will be to glorify the Son, the Word of God Himself (John 1:1).

It is important to see the Spirit's role in Jesus's prayer to His Father, because what Jesus continues to pray has much of its focus in this symbiotic relation between the Word and the Spirit when Jesus departs. Notice:

> I have revealed you to those whom you gave me out of the world. They were yours; you gave them to me and they have obeyed your word. Now they know that everything you have given me comes from you. For I gave them the words you gave me and they accepted them. They knew with certainty that I came from you, and they believed that you sent me. (John 17:6–8)

Here we see Jesus reflecting again on those whom the Father had given Him. One of the things Jesus did with them is He gave them *the words* the Father had given Him, and they accepted them. That is, Jesus taught His disciples what His Father had said—"Every word that proceeds from the mouth of God"—and His disciples accepted them. Notice also:

> I have given them your word and the world has hated them, for they are not of the world any more than I am of the world. . . . Sanctify them by the truth; your word is truth. . . . My prayer is not for them alone. I pray also for those who will believe in me through their message . . . (14, 17, 20)

The progression here is again important. Jesus gave the Father's words to the disciples. As we have seen, they accepted those words, and the world hated them because of it. Jesus prays that His disciples would be sanctified, that is, set apart "by the truth." The truth that will set them apart is, Jesus says, those very words. And Jesus has more to say, which the Spirit will give to them.

Surely the disciples who were privy to this prayer of their Lord would have seen, if not at that moment, eventually, that the truth by which they were to be set apart was the truth that came to them through the "Spirit of truth." It is the truth, more specifically, that comes by way of the Word and the Spirit.

And then Jesus utters in one clause what is, for us, the foundation of all that we know and believe. He says to His Father that He is praying "for those who will believe in me *through their message*." The word translated "message" here is the Greek word *logos*.

As we have already seen, *Logos* is the word that John uses in this Gospel for Christ Himself, and it is also the word that is used for Scripture. Those who now trust in Christ do so "through their word," the word that is wrought by the Spirit who has been sent to testify of and glorify the Word Himself.

The fact that Jesus prays "for those who will believe in me through their message" should be an inexpressible comfort to us. But, as important, Jesus recognizes that when He departs, there will be those who will believe in Him *through the word* that the disciples will be given. That word will be given through the Spirit of truth, who will come to glorify the Word Himself, and who will bring to mind all that Jesus said to His disciples. The disciples, by the Spirit, will give that word to His people, to the church.

In this Upper Room Discourse, as the disciples are given a flood of new information to prepare them for their lives apart from their Savior's bodily presence, Jesus has shown them the link between Him, His Father, and the Spirit. That link will include them, because the Spirit will come to continue the ministry of the Word that Jesus Himself had been giving them.

The Word and the Spirit will go on, in the ministry of the disciples, because the Spirit will be sent to them for that very purpose. Thus, the sword that we take up for our spiritual battle is the sword *of the Spirit, which is the word of God.* It is the Father's Word, given to the Son and then revealed to the disciples through the Holy Spirit.

There is much more that could be discussed as we think about the relation of the Word and the Spirit, and about how our Savior thought about and taught about those important truths. Enough has been said, however, for us to recognize the gloriously deep and complex tapestry of truths that the Lord gives to us in His Word.

The Lord's view of Scripture was that it was from the very mouth of His heavenly Father. He defined His entire ministry by what Scripture said to and about Him (see, for example, Matt 26:53–54; Luke 24:25–27). And He told His disciples how that ministry would continue when He departed. The "Word ministry," Jesus told them, will be the "Spirit ministry." Scripture is, and will continue to be, "God-Spirited."

When Paul commands us to take "the sword of the Spirit, which is the word of God," He is expressing nothing more and nothing less than what his Savior expressed. He is recognizing that the cosmic war is fought as the enemies of Christ are subdued with "the breath of His mouth." He is recognizing that "the breath of His mouth" is nothing less than the Spirit-wrought word of God, which Jesus Himself recognized as defining His own ministry.

When that earthly ministry was done, Jesus sent His promised Spirit so that the words that He had given to His disciples, which were themselves from the Father, might be recalled and written, so that there would be "those who believe in me *through their message*." The sword of the Spirit, which is the word of God, is the only weapon we have, and the only one we need, to engage the spiritual battle persuasively. A persuasive apologetic can only be so as it is focused on the Word and the Spirit.

As with Christ, so also with us. The battle cannot be fought without our sword; without it, we have nothing with which to strike Christ's enemies. However, with the sword—since it is the sword *of the Spirit* and is the *word of God*—like Jesus in the wilderness, we can engage the apologetic battle. And we can trust that, through the Spirit and by the Word, some will be subdued and persuaded to bow the knee to Christ, to whom all authority in heaven and on earth has now been given.

Now that we have seen that the Spirit and the Word are inextricably linked, we need to look a little more closely at each of them individually in order to appreciate their distinct roles in apologetics and persuasion.

THE AUTHORITY OF HOLY SCRIPTURE

In one sense, we are now returning to the place where we began. As we thought about our Divine Persuader in chapter 1, we recognized that, from the beginning, He condescended *to speak*. This is no insignificant event. Of all the things that distinguish human beings from the rest of creation—and there are many—one of the most obvious distinctions is language. Some animals are able to mimic a kind of "back and forth" between them, but nothing else in creation can employ the complexities of language that human beings use. And we typically grasp our language with relative ease.

This is the case because God chose to condescend to us, in part, *by speaking.* Included in His speaking is our ability to understand, and to respond with that same speech. The mystery of human language has its genesis in Genesis. The Lord spoke to us, and He made us to respond to His speech by speaking. Any words we speak assume, in the first place, His speech to us. We speak because He first spoke to us. Speech, in other words, is included in the "bridge" that the Lord built between Himself and us, so that He could be our God and we could be His people. It is the bedrock of any and all persuasion.

We also saw that so many of the occasions where "the word of the Lord" comes or appears in the Old Testament were likely occasions where someone was present to speak and to act. That "someone," it seems, was the "Word" Himself, the second person of the Trinity. As the Lord condescends to speak, the focus of that condescension, and of that speech, is in the Son of God.

He is the only begotten Son, who is sent by the Father to establish a relationship with His people throughout redemptive history. As we have just seen, once the Son's earthly mission is completed, He continues His ministry of speaking by sending the Spirit. The Spirit comes and He speaks the "much more" (John 16:12) that Christ wanted to say to His disciples. As He speaks, the words of Christ are written by His Spirit-chosen instruments, so that His people might "believe in me through *their* message."

There is, therefore, an unbroken and unbreakable connection between that original, condescending speech of God "in the beginning" and the speech of God which we have now as the "sword of the Spirit." There has never been a time when human beings have been on earth and when God has not spoken. He has always communicated to human beings.

He tells us who He is, who we are, and how we are to think about Him, ourselves, and everything else He has made. To use Paul's categories (2 Tim 3:16), He communicates to teach us, to rebuke us, and to train us in righteousness. His word is a lamp for our feet and a light for our path (Ps 119:105). Without it, we walk through life in darkness and without a guide. If the Lord does not speak, we are blind; we grope in the dark without any light.

From the very beginning, the Lord's word has been under attack. Satan's ploy with Adam and Eve, subtle though it was at first, was a direct attack on what the Lord had said to them. The Lord assured our first parents that if they ate from the forbidden tree, they would die. Satan audaciously contradicted what the Lord had said: "You will not certainly die!" (Gen 3:4).

As we noted above, Adam and Eve were seduced into thinking that they did not live by every word that proceeded from the Lord's mouth. They became convinced that they could live *better* by listening to the voice of the serpent. As it turned out, it was the Lord's voice alone that proved to be true and accurate.

The promise from the Lord was that they would die, and they did. Satan's voice, from that time forth and forever, is the voice of a liar (John 8:44). The Lord's voice, because it is His, from the beginning, is the voice of truth. It comes from the Spirit of truth. It proceeds from His very mouth.

During the time of the Reformation in the sixteenth century, the word of God was again under attack. This attack was not as audacious as the serpent's. It was much more subtle, and thus more dangerous, because it came from within the church.

There were many reasons why the church was in deep need of reform by the time of the sixteenth century. The tactics of the church bureaucracy were causing pain to the poorest of its members. The church was more concerned about its own financial growth than it was about the spiritual growth of those within its doors. Clearly, it was time for the church to be re-formed.

The issues surrounding the reformation of the corruption in the church had their focus under two headings. They have been designated as the "formal principle" and the "material principle." Other issues were discussed and debated, but these two principles were the primary initial focus of the reformation of the church. The "material principle" had to do with the specific "matter" that needed to be clarified and re-formed. The material principle was the principle of justification by faith *alone* (*sola fide*).

The church had lapsed into thinking that our right standing in the presence of God somehow depended, at least in part, on what we ourselves had done and could do. So, even though the church during that time would agree that our justification was by faith, it would not agree that our justification was by faith *alone*.

The Reformation made clear that whatever we do in our relationship with God earns us *nothing* with respect to our salvation. Our justification—that which puts us in a proper relationship to God—can only be by faith *alone*, because only God could accomplish what we could not. Justification could not be by faith plus works of charity, or any other works. Salvation was not a cooperative enterprise. This was the material principle that sparked the Reformation.

Important for our specific purposes in this section, however, is the "formal principle" of the Reformation. This principle is primary, because it grounds and founds the "material principle." It is from the formal principle that all other principles are derived. The formal principle provides the "form" from which the "matter" is described, defined, and properly understood.

In other words, the "formal" question during this time was something like this: How do we know what justification is and how it is applied to us? At the beginning of the sixteenth century, the common view was that it was the church that determined these things. The church was the "formal principle" and thus it decided all of the "material principles" of the faith. Christians just needed to trust the church in these matters.

The Reformers rightly rejected this idea. One of the reasons that the church had become so corrupt was just *because* it was claiming to be the ultimate authority. It acknowledged Scripture as *an* authority, but only within the context of the ultimate authority of the church's tradition. It was the church that decided what Scripture was, and what it meant.

More specifically, it was the hierarchy of the church that decided for the rest of the church how to think about the word of God and what it teaches. Since the church claimed ultimate authority, it was not accountable to anyone else. And since the church, like everything else, is made up of sinners (even if redeemed), it was bound to become corrupt.

As the Reformation of the church moved through the sixteenth and into the seventeenth century, various creeds and confessions were written so that those who were "protesting" against the corruption of the church—those called "Protestants"—might be unified in their re-formed and re-forming beliefs. One of the most magnificent creeds written during the seventeenth century was the *Westminster Confession of Faith*. As we think about "the sword of the Spirit, which is the word of God," this Confession's statements on Scripture are of immense value.

Chapter 1 of this Confession is entitled "Of the Holy Scripture." It is important to recognize why this is the first chapter. The reason this was the first chapter was because the writers knew that the "formal principle" needed to be set out before any other "material principles" could be addressed. We need to know what Scripture is and how to think about it before we can get to its teachings on various topics.

After discussing Scripture's necessity, and its proper contents, including the books included and those to be excluded, the Confession moves, in section 4 of this first chapter, to the central topic of Scripture's *authority*. In a concise and penetrating way, it explains what scriptural authority means:

> The authority of the Holy Scripture, for which it ought to be believed, and obeyed, dependeth not upon the testimony of any man, or Church; but wholly upon God (who is truth itself) the author thereof: and therefore it is to be received, because it is the Word of God.[2]

---

2. *The Westminster Confession of Faith*, chapter 1, section 4 (Oak Harbor, WA: Logos Research Systems, Inc., 1996).

The flow of thought in this section is of great importance if we are to understand it properly. First, it states that Holy Scripture should be "believed and obeyed" because of its authority. This will be an important point as we think about the use of Scripture in our apologetics and in persuasion.

The words that are given to us in our Bibles are not simply the thoughts of those who wrote down those words. Because of *whose* they are, they carry the Lord's own authority. Surely, it would be wrong to "believe and obey" them if they were only the words of men, or anything but the Lord's own words. This follows from Paul's description of Scripture as "the sword of the Spirit." Scripture carries the authority of the Holy Spirit Himself, which is the full authority of God.

But how did Holy Scripture acquire this authority? The first answer is put in the negative. Scripture's authority "dependeth not upon the testimony of any man, or Church." Given the various ways the church had become corrupt, we can see why this denial is so crucial. It might be worth pausing for a minute to let this truth soak in.

Why do you believe your Bible? There could be a number of proper answers to that question. Maybe you were raised in a Christian home and you believe your Bible because you were taught to believe it from your youth. Maybe, like Timothy, your faith was passed down from Christians in your own family (2 Tim 1:5).[3]

Or maybe your conversion to Christ was more sudden than that. Maybe you lived a large part of your life apart from Christ and then, when someone explained the gospel to you, you trusted Christ, and your life radically changed forever. Maybe you believe your Bible because the one who explained the gospel to you also began to explain what the Bible meant in its various books and passages.

Or maybe you believe your Bible because you attend a church that believes the Bible and you listen, week after week, to your minister explain

---

3. For more on why we believe the Bible, see K. Scott Oliphint, *Know Why You Believe* (Grand Rapids: Zondervan, 2016), especially chapter 1.

the texts on which he preaches. You have fellowship with others who believe the Bible, and you all grow together in Christ in the context of worship, prayer, and fellowship.

These examples, though legitimate, are not exactly what the Confession is addressing. It is attempting to help us see why the Scripture is our ultimate *authority*. Even if we believe the Bible because of our family, that fact shouldn't lead us to ascribe *ultimate* authority to a family member. We may consult them for help in understanding Scripture, but, as Christians, we wouldn't do that because we deemed them to have the ultimate authority of God Himself.

The same is true for the church. We may gain much of our understanding of Scripture from the minister in preaching and from other various ministries in the church. Even so, we should not think that our ministers are given any ultimate authority. Such authority is what cults are made of. We may, and should, trust our ministers in their interpretation of Scripture. They were trained and called for that very purpose. But our trust should never be unqualified and absolute.

This section is telling us that it is not proper to think the authority of Holy Scripture depends on some other person or on the church, as important as the church is. The point here is sweeping in its scope and should be read that way. To put the point more starkly, there is not one human being or a collection of human beings, no evidence or collection of evidences, not one institution—not even the church—on which the authority of Holy Scripture depends.

We saw above that Jesus provided a way for His disciples to remember what He had said and to communicate those words to the church. In that sense, the ones to whom the Holy Spirit was given in this unique way continued the authority that Christ Himself had in His communication of the word of God.

But we should not confuse that authority with those to whom it was given. Scripture is not "the sword of Paul" or "the sword of Peter" or of Matthew, Mark, Luke, or John. The word of God is the "sword *of the Spirit*" because any authority that Paul or Peter or any other writer of Holy

Scripture had, he had only because of the Holy Spirit Himself, who was sent by the Father to glorify the Son (John 16:13–14). The authority of Holy Scripture, then, does not depend on any person. As a matter of fact, there is *nothing* in creation on which the authority of Scripture depends.

On what, then, does Scripture's authority depend? After telling us on what the authority of Scripture does *not* depend, this section of the Confession turns to the positive. If we take out the negative clauses, it reads this way: "The authority of Holy Scripture, for which it ought to be believed and obeyed depends . . . wholly upon God (who is truth itself) the author thereof." This is a remarkably succinct and powerful statement. Given what we discussed in the previous section of this chapter, however, it should not surprise us.

The Confession is tasked with explaining the Protestant position on various doctrines. As we have already seen, the Roman church during this time had made it clear that one's trust in Scripture depended, first, on one's trust in the church. Christians were taught to trust the church *in order to* trust Scripture. This order of dependence turns out to be devastating to Scripture's authority.

It is devastating, because if there is something else (other than Christ Himself) that we put our trust in, *first of all*, in order to trust Scripture, then the first thing we trust is, by definition, our ultimate authority; we trust Scripture *because* we trust something else first. If we trust Scripture's authority *because* the church tells us we can, then the church could just as easily tell us what cannot be trusted in Scripture. Or, more concretely, the church has the authority to determine which books are included in Scripture and which are not. This is the reason why the Roman church's Bible is different from the Protestant Bible. It is the issue of ultimate authority.[4]

---

4. As we will note below, the notion of Scripture's ultimate authority is sometimes called its "self-attestation" or "self-authentication," and that is what 1.4 of the *Confession* is affirming. For more on this, see K. Scott Oliphint, "Because It Is the Word of God," in David B. Garner, *Did God Really Say?: Affirming the Truthfulness and Trustworthiness of Scripture* (Phillipsburg, NJ: Presbyterian & Reformed, 2012), 1–22.

When the Confession says that the authority of Holy Scripture depends "wholly upon God" who is "the author thereof," we can see that it is echoing what Jesus Himself affirmed. Jesus believed that what was written in Scripture was "every word that proceeds out of the mouth of God" (Matt 4:4 NASB).

At no point did Jesus even hint that His trust in Scripture's authority depended on the synagogue and its affirmation of the books of Scripture, or on leaders within Israel, or even on the prophets themselves! Jesus defined His entire life and ministry according to what Scripture said to and about Him (see Matt 26:53–54; Luke 24:25–27). He did that because what Scripture said to Him was "from the mouth" of His heavenly Father.

But Jesus also recognized the authority of what He Himself said, and the responsibility of those who heard Him to believe it. In one of His many debates with the Jews, He made this clear:

> Jesus said to them, "If God were your Father, you would love me, for I have come here from God. I have not come on my own; God sent me. Why is my language not clear to you? Because you are unable to hear what I say. You belong to your father, the devil, and you want to carry out your father's desires. He was a murderer from the beginning, not holding to the truth, for there is no truth in him. When he lies, he speaks his native language, for he is a liar and the father of lies. Yet because I tell the truth, you do not believe me! Can any of you prove me guilty of sin? If I am telling the truth, why don't you believe me? *Whoever belongs to God hears what God says. The reason you do not hear is that you do not belong to God.*" (John 8:42–47, emphasis mine)

Notice that Jesus says the Jews are "unable to hear" what He says. Then He explains to them why they do not hear Him. They are not children of Abraham, as they supposed. Instead, they are of their father, the devil. That is why Jesus's own language is not clear to them. Jesus is not speaking in an unclear way. The problem is with the listeners; their language is the language of their father, the language of lies. Jesus says that they "want to carry out" the father's lies.

Notice how Jesus then equates what He says with what God says: "Whoever belongs to God hears what *God says*. The reason you do not hear is that you do not belong to God." This is stunning in its scope. Jesus is affirming that what He says, God says. His words to them are the words of God. The reason they cannot hear Jesus is that God's words cannot be understood by those who do not belong to God. If they did belong to God, they would hear Jesus and understand what He means when He speaks.

In other words, the Jews ought to believe what He says *because what He says is God's word*. But they cannot believe; they won't believe. They do not belong to God. The point that Jesus is making is that what is needed to *hear and believe* God's Word has everything to do with the one(s) who should believe; the problem is never with God's Word itself. God's Word is sufficient in itself. He is the author, and our response should be to trust and believe.

The people who wrote the *Westminster Confession* were well aware that, throughout history, the Lord chose various men to write His Word (see Heb 1:1). And those who wrote exhibited various traits of their own personalities and training in their writings. But, as we have seen, what they wrote is, in the end, *theopneustos*—God-breathed. They wrote as men who were "carried along by the Holy Spirit." Even as they retained their own style of writing and their own personalities, the words written were God's Word.

From Genesis to Revelation, therefore, Scripture has one primary author: God Himself. Even as He used men to write, they wrote *His* word, not theirs. They write what He wants the church throughout history to know. What they write "proceeds from the mouth of God." This is what Jesus knew, and it is what guided His entire life. It is what we are meant to know as well, and it should guide our entire lives.

The concluding clauses in this section of the Confession can sound rather stark at first glance. Given that God is *the* author of Holy Scripture, what should our response be? "And therefore it is to be received, because it is the Word of God." This entire section has been leading up to this final point.

The verb used here is intentional and central: We are to "receive" the Scripture because it is God's very word. To receive is a passive act. It is what we do when we are *given* something. A true gift is not determined by us. We do not make it, buy it, work for it, or decide if it is a gift or not. A true gift is *received*. So it is with Scripture. The Christian's responsibility is to take Scripture for what it is, a gift from the Lord to His people.

The *reason* we are obliged to receive Scripture is because "it is the Word of God." This is the proper place to introduce a somewhat technical term that makes all the difference when we think about the character of God's Word to us. It informs our apologetics and its persuasion. The term is *self-authentication*.

To better understand this term, we need to go back to the sixteenth century again for just a moment. At the time of the Reformation, the general view of the church and its members was that Scripture is what it is and says what it says *because* of what the church has declared. In this case, the Word of God is "church-authenticated."

The Reformers understood this. As they were seeking to reform the church, they recognized that their re-formed view of Scripture took away this now-standard view of its authentication. If the church does not authenticate Scripture and give Scripture its authority, who does?

Here is how John Calvin, a sixteenth-century reformer, answered that question:

> It is utterly vain, then, to pretend that the power of judging Scripture so lies with the church that its certainty depends upon churchly assent. Thus, while the church receives and gives its seal of approval to the Scriptures, it does not thereby render authentic what is otherwise doubtful or controversial. But because the church recognizes Scripture to be the truth of its own God, as a pious duty it unhesitatingly venerates Scripture. As to their question—How can we be assured that this has sprung from God unless we have recourse to the decree

of the church?—it is as if someone asked: Whence will we learn to distinguish light from darkness, white from black, sweet from bitter? Indeed, Scripture exhibits fully as clear evidence of its own truth as white and black things do of their color, or sweet and bitter things do of their taste.[5]

Calvin's analogies here are helpful. "Self-authentication" is analogous to the sweetness of honey or the light of the sun. If someone needs to know if honey is sweet, all that is needed is to taste it. If someone needs to know if the light of the sun is shining, all that is needed is to look. Nothing is needed for honey to be sweet, or for the sun to shine. Sweetness and light are "self-authenticated" in honey and the sun. Our taste of honey, or look at the sun, simply confirm what is already there; they do not *establish* what is there.

These analogies help us to see that "self-authentication" is a characteristic that is attached to Scripture itself. It is *not* a characteristic that belongs to *us*. Scripture needs nothing but itself in order to be authoritative, just as honey needs nothing but itself in order to be sweet. But just because Scripture's authority is "self-authenticated" does not mean we will automatically believe it. More is needed.

This view of Scripture provides a host of helpful cues to our apologetics and our hope for persuasion. We will look at those shortly. In the meantime, two more implications of Scripture's self-authentication need to be mentioned in conclusion.

THE SPIRIT OF PERSUASION

Scripture's self-authentication means that its authority is intrinsic to itself. Since Scripture is "every word that proceeds from the mouth of God,"

---

5. John Calvin, *Institutes of the Christian Religion*, ed. John T. McNeill, trans. Ford Lewis Battles, vol. 1, The Library of Christian Classics (Louisville: Westminster John Knox, 2011), 76.

since it is "God-breathed," the words in Scripture carry the authority of their Author. In other words, it is the *Author* that gives Scripture its *authority*. This might lead us initially to think that this view of Scripture leaves no room for arguments. If Scripture is self-authenticated, then nothing can be said in its defense.

The writers of the Confession anticipated that reaction. In the next section, section 5, they spelled out some categories that could be included as arguments for Scripture's character. Note:

> We may be moved and induced by the testimony of the Church to an high and reverent esteem of the Holy Scripture. And the heavenliness of the matter, the efficacy of the doctrine, the majesty of the style, the consent of all the parts, the scope of the whole (which is, to give all glory to God), the full discovery it makes of the only way of man's salvation, the many other incomparable excellencies, and the entire perfection thereof, are arguments whereby it does abundantly evidence itself to be the Word of God . . . [6]

Given the fact that Scripture attests to its own authority, some of the best arguments we can give for Scripture's character are in Scripture itself.

The reason these arguments can be effective is precisely *because* Scripture's authority is given in each and every one of them. If we speak to someone about "the heavenliness of the matter," or of "the efficacy of the doctrine" of Scripture, they will be confronted with the self-authenticating authority of Scripture by those very arguments. If we show them "the consent of all the parts," or "the scope of the whole," they come face to face with God's own authority in each and every word given.

But what effect does this self-authenticating Word have when people are confronted with it? When the Lord spoke to the prophet Isaiah about His Word, he put it this way:

---

6. *The Westminster Confession of Faith*, chapter 1, section 5 (Oak Harbor, WA: Logos Research Systems, Inc., 1996).

As the rain and the snow come down from heaven, and do not return to it without watering the earth and making it bud and flourish, so that it yields seed for the sower and bread for the eater, so is my word that goes out from my mouth: It will not return to me empty, but will accomplish what I desire and achieve the purpose for which I sent it. (Isa 55:10–11)

Notice that when the word of God goes out, it always accomplishes the Lord's own purposes and it achieves what He desires. In other words, there is no argument given, when its content is God's own truth, that is ever given in vain, or that is "unsuccessful." When the Lord's Word is given, He makes sure that it will accomplish exactly what He desires for it.

When we are involved in a persuasive defense of Christianity, that defense must always include the truth that God has revealed to us. There are various ways to communicate those truths—more ways than we could ever hope to know—but our goal must be that people hear the truth of God's own Word in our defense of Christianity. When they do, that Word will be the means the Lord uses to do as He pleases. In that sense, communicating God's truth to people is *always* successful, even if the response is negative. We will have more to say about this in later chapters.

We have already established and seen that there is an unbreakable link between the Word of God and the Holy Spirit. That link has radical implications when we think about the matter of persuasion. As we will discuss later, there are various things that we can think and do in order to defend the faith persuasively, and to communicate in a way that might serve to bring others into our discussion, rather than push them away from it.

But, for all of that, the last part of section 5 in the Confession has to be our guiding principle of persuasion. Just after the material quoted above, section 5 concludes this way:

Yet notwithstanding, our full persuasion and assurance of the infallible truth and divine authority thereof, is from the inward work of the Holy Spirit bearing witness by and with the Word in our hearts.[7]

There can be no arguments given, or persuasion applied, that, in and of themselves, will *guarantee* a positive response. If that were the case, then everyone would have believed in and trusted Jesus. Surely, His arguments were persuasive and unassailable.

As the Confession makes clear here, there is only one avenue of true and *effective* persuasion. "Our full persuasion . . . is from the inward work of the Holy Spirit." That is, even as we recognize that God's Word always accomplishes its divine purpose, that purpose is not always that someone be converted. Jesus made this clear to His listeners: "The Spirit gives life; the flesh counts for nothing. The words I have spoken to you—they are full of the Spirit and life. Yet there are some of you who do not believe" (John 6:63–64). The words Jesus spoke "are full of the Spirit and life." They are able to persuade. Yet, there were those listening who would not believe. Jesus tells us why they would not believe:

> "Yet there are some of you who do not believe." For Jesus had known from the beginning which of them did not believe and who would betray him. He went on to say, "This is why I told you that no one can come to me unless the Father has enabled them." From this time many of his disciples turned back and no longer followed him. (John 6:64–66)

There are some who would not believe. Jesus tells them that they cannot come to Him "unless the Father has enabled" them.

In other words, even as Jesus's own words are "Spirit and life," the same Spirit who bears witness "by and with the Word" must bear that witness "in our hearts" if we are going to believe and trust in Christ.

---

7. Ibid.

We saw in the first chapter that God is the Divine Persuader. He comes down and He speaks to us. In this chapter, we have been able to dive a little deeper in order to see how Scripture speaks to us in our current context. Now that Christ has completed His work, has ascended to the Father, and has sent the Spirit, Divine Persuasion and our defense of Christianity comes, when it does, by way of the Spirit bearing witness by and with the Word of God in our hearts.

The Divine Persuader remains the Divine Persuader throughout history:

> In the past God spoke to our ancestors through the prophets at many times and in various ways, but in these last days he has spoken to us by his Son, whom he appointed heir of all things, and through whom also he made the universe. (Heb 1:1–2)

When the Son speaks, and the Spirit bears witness to that word in our hearts, we are divinely persuaded. Without the Word and the Spirit together, there will be no true and *full* persuasion, even as there will be no real defense of the faith.

Our responsibility, then, in apologetics and in persuasion, is to take "the sword of the Spirit, which is the word of God," and to communicate that in a defense of Christianity as persuasively as we are able. When we do that faithfully, we have done all that can humanly be done. When we do that faithfully, we can be confident that the Lord's word will never fail; there is no possibility it will not accomplish His divine purposes. When we do that faithfully, we pray and hope that the Word and Spirit will be applied to human hearts so that the enemies of Christ will continue to be subdued, as the Father continues to make His Son's enemies a footstool for His feet.

In part 2 of our study, we will focus more directly on three central aspects of persuasion, in order to think about their use in our defense of Christianity. As we do, we will need to remember that God alone, through His Spirit, can change human hearts. But we will also need to remember that He changes hearts by way of the truth of the Word and the Spirit. As Word and Spirit work together, in our apologetics and persuasion, the Lord will draw people to Himself. As we defend the faith persuasively, the Lord continues to build a footstool for His Son. Those who, like us, were once His enemies, are subdued by His grace and come to Him by faith alone.

PART 2

PARTS AND PRINCIPLES
of Apologetics and Persuasion

FOUR

ETHOS

God is the first and primary Persuader. He speaks, we hear Him, and we speak as well. Not only so, but He is the original Apologist. He persuades and He defends His truth by way of His Word. That Word, which is His very speech, has its focus in the Word Himself, the second person of the Trinity, who "connected" Himself to us by becoming one of us, and who persuaded us by drawing us to Himself.

What we hope to do in the next three chapters is to begin to merge together the previous three, as the themes of those chapters apply to us. That is, as we have said, we want to think about how the *Word of God* can be communicated by us in order to *defend* the Christian faith in a *persuasive* manner. Now that we recognize God as the Persuader and Defender, centrally through *His Word*, we can see that our own attempts to defend and persuade are themselves attempts to "image" what God Himself does. We attempt to persuade in our defense, through our words, because God Himself has done so in and by His Word and Spirit.

ETHOS, PATHOS, AND *LOGOS*

In the past, in the West, it was thought that the best foundation for education was in the so-called liberal arts. "Liberal" arts were so named because they were meant to apply to "free" citizens. They were also meant to provide for free citizens an education that would prepare students for a robust and productive life in society.

It would be useful, perhaps, to trace this initial emphasis on the liberal arts to current-day trends in education. Anecdotally, at least, there seems to be far less emphasis on the liberal arts these days and much more emphasis on practical arts—arts designed to enhance the possibility of employment. This practical emphasis is understandable, even commendable. But one of the negative consequences of a practical emphasis is that one can proceed apace through every program of education, including a doctorate, and never undertake the type of study that used to be touted as foundational for any true, meaningful, and lasting education.

The current practical bent, it seems, does not bode well for any discipline, theology included, in which a premium is placed on the value of the word and of thinking. An education that is focused on practice may produce employment, but it may also produce a society wherein reading, thinking, studying, meditating, synthesizing, and persuading are virtually absent. Witness, for example, any televised political debate. No matter which side of the political spectrum one is on, to call what happens on television within an hour or two a "debate" is, from the perspective of history, difficult to take seriously.

One of the great advantages of an emphasis on the liberal arts is that it takes the art of communication very seriously. It highlights not only the central importance of *words* for communication, but, as we will see below, it focuses on the proper rules and uses of words so that communication between people can be more uniform and more easily understood. As we can see, this emphasis blends well with our own concern for persuasion in apologetics.

In the "old days" (and by that, I mean a few thousand years ago), a student's curriculum would initially consist of three subjects, called the *trivium*. These three needed to be learned in their particular order, as each would build on the one prior to it. The first thing a student would be required to learn in the *trivium* was grammar. In this discipline, students learned the proper way to understand languages (as well as other disciplines). Because there are rules to every language, it is important to understand and apply those rules in order to grasp and apply the basics of communication.

The second subject matter that students would take up was called dialectic or logic. In this subject, students would begin to build on the rules of language and work on proper modes of reasoning. Dialectic, or logic, we can see, presupposes the rules of language; in that way, it depended on an adequate understanding of grammar.

Once the basic rules of speech and communication were understood, students were taught to think about how best to synthesize and bring together various sentences and propositions. Students would learn rules of induction and deduction, rules of arguments and other modes of reasoning. In that way, they could be equipped not simply to evaluate grammatical rules, but to judge whether certain statements or collections of statements were plausible, implausible, true, or false.

The last of the three basic subjects of the *trivium* was rhetoric. In rhetoric, students would begin to apply their knowledge of grammar and logic to proper ways of speaking and communicating. In this subject, the focus was on oratory in such a way that an audience could be properly informed, motivated, or *persuaded.*

In this and the next two chapters, we hope to work through some key biblical and theological principles that will help us recognize the interface between defending the Christian faith and persuasion. In order to do that, we need to be introduced to the three aspects of persuasion, all of which are central to a Christian apologetic as well.

The Greek philosopher Aristotle (384–322 BC) set forth three "kinds" or categories that were present in any and every persuasive discourse:

> Of the modes of persuasion furnished by the spoken word there are three kinds. The first kind depends on the personal character [*ethos*] of the speaker; the second kind on putting the audience into a certain

frame of mind [*pathos*]; the third on proof, or apparent proof, provided by the words of the speech itself [*logos*].[1]

So, as Aristotle laid it out, persuasion consists of three central aspects—*ethos*, *pathos*, and *logos*. A bit of explanation is needed for each of these.

In order to see them in their proper biblical and theological context, we will take these three in turn in the next three chapters. In this chapter, we will set our sights on the importance of *the person* and his character (*ethos*), in apologetics and persuasion. In the next chapter, we will focus on the *pathos* of persuasion and apologetics, that is, on those to whom we speak, our audience (whether one or many). In the final chapter, we will conclude where we began. We will return again to our focus on the *logos*, that is, the importance of the *words* or message which we speak and use in apologetics and persuasion.

OUR UNIVERSAL *ETHOS*: IMAGING GOD

Ethos has its focus in a person's *character*. With respect to persuasion, it asks the question, "What about *this person* supports the ideas I am supposed to consider or accept?" Put negatively, a person whose character lacks credibility will be, to that extent, hard-pressed to convince someone that his own views are credible.

Before we discuss the *differences* between those who are in Christ and those who are not—differences that are the backdrop of persuasion and apologetics—we should remind ourselves of the *unity* that humanity was meant to display. This unity is the baseline character—the universal *ethos*—of all of God's human creatures. It is also the basis of our humanity and forms the foundation for our theology of persuasion in apologetics.

---

1. Aristotle, "Rhetorica," *The Basic Works of Aristotle*, ed. Richard McKeon (New York: Random House, 2009), 1601.

We have already seen in chapter 1 that our creation in the image of God was, in part, the "connection" or "link" that the Lord provided for human beings so that we could know Him and responsibly obey Him. The animals were given commands when they were created. Those commands, however, were going to be fulfilled "naturally." They were not given commands that they were held accountable to obey.

When God created Adam, and Eve from Adam, they were given identical commands as the animals (see Gen 1:22, 28). They were, unlike the animals, given commands for which they were *responsible* before God. Adam was told to name the animals (Gen 2:19), which was a clear indication of Adam's rule over the animals, a rule that could only be rightly carried out under God's sovereign rule. Eve was made, from Adam, as equally the image of God, and as one who would help Adam and who would be "one flesh" with him (Gen 2:24). No animals were given such gifts and responsibilities.

We learn from those initial days of creation that to be the "image of God," as Adam and Eve were, means to be "like" God in the relationship that He has established. For example, in the days of creation leading up to the creation of Adam and Eve, Moses tells us that "God *called* the light 'day,' and the darkness he *called* 'night'" (Gen 1:5). He also tells us that "God *called* the vault 'sky'" (Gen 1:8), and that "God *called* the dry ground 'land,' and the gathered waters he *called* 'seas'" (Gen 1:10, emphasis mine).

After God creates the animals, however, He brings them to Adam to name: ". . . and whatever the man *called* each living creature, that was its name" (Gen 2:19). This is a clear signal that Adam was meant to "image" God. God *called* the light, day, and the darkness, night; He called the vault, sky, etc.

Then God brings the animals to Adam, and whatever Adam *called* each animal, that was its name. The authority that God alone had, in calling various aspects of creation what He wanted to name them, He gave to Adam as He brought Adam the animals to name. Thus, in "imaging" God, Adam has authority over creation, but always under the sovereign authority of God. Adam's "naming" was like God's "naming"; it was meant to image something of who God is.

In "imaging" God, Adam and Eve were told to "subdue" the earth (Gen 1:28). This aspect of "subduing" can provide for us a large picture window through which we can view what it means to be God's image, both before and after the fall into sin.

The responsibility to "subdue" God's creation, under His sovereign rule, requires a complexity of abilities and gifts that are, in the end, mysterious. In order to subdue the earth and to rule over it, under God, human beings must be self-conscious in a way that animals could never be. They must be able to speak, to think, to conceive thoughts, to analyze and synthesize a multitude of data and concepts.

They must be creative themselves, under God, as they utilize aspects of creation for the good of creation and of other human beings. The scientific discipline of medicine, to use just one example, when properly carried out, is a wonderful example of what it means for human beings to "subdue" God's creation.

Our recent pandemic is a good example of this. Within a year of the novel Coronavirus, which appeared in 2019, researchers developed a few vaccines that would protect almost everyone from its harmful effects. Though the vaccines were rapidly developed, the research for the vaccine was decades old. For the mRNA vaccines, for example, researchers had been studying how our bodies' cells make proteins that trigger an immune response to viruses. Instead of injecting dead cells from the virus itself, the mRNA vaccine can trigger an immune response from our cells without needing the virus. This is just one example of taking what we know of God's creation and using it—subduing it—in order to diminish the ill effects of creation, which themselves are a result of sin (Rom 8:18–22).

Without the gifts and abilities that are ours by virtue of being made in God's image, it would not be possible to "rule over the fish in the sea and the birds in the sky . . . and over all the creatures that move along the ground" (Gen 1:26). Since Adam and Eve were given such gifts, they were placed in the garden so that they could "*work* it and *take care* of it"

(Gen 2:15). All of this, for Adam and Eve, we should remember, was to be done before there was any sin in the world.

Central to being the image of God, therefore, is this "subduing" of creation, under God, and all of the multifaceted aspects of human beings that subduing requires. We could think of this "imaging" like this: when God began to create, He spoke, and it was. He said, "Let there be . . ." and there was.

But we also see that the Lord used aspects of creation to create other things. He created the animals and fish from the dust of the ground (Gen 2:19). From that dust, He also created Adam, and then distinguished him by breathing into him the breath of life (Gen 2:7). From Adam's side, the Lord created Eve (Gen 2:21–22).

In all of these acts, the Lord is using His own creation in order to create new things. In that sense, the Lord is "working and taking care of" that which He has made, extending its potential by His sovereign, creating power. He is subduing and ruling over creation in order to cultivate it and supernaturally to demonstrate its potential.

All subduing that human beings do should be accomplished under God, and according to His character. The rule that God gave to Adam and Eve was meant to "image" God's own rule. Like God, it was a rule that was designed to cultivate God's good creation, to demonstrate its seemingly unlimited potential. As God took dust and made animals and Adam, so also, in an analogous way, Adam and Eve were to cultivate the ground, the plants, and the animals in order more fully to show forth the goodness of what God had made, and thus God's own goodness.

As we are all too aware, the good "subduing" that Adam and Eve were supposed to accomplish turned horribly bad. Instead of subduing the animals, the serpent subdued Adam and Eve. Satan used the serpent to subdue the goodness of God's creation, including the goodness of Adam and Eve, and to turn it to ruin.

As we see Adam and Eve "pass the buck" after their sin, we see the sinful "subduing series" in action. Adam says Eve made him do it; Eve says the serpent made her do it (Gen 3:12–13). The fact of the matter is that, instead of subduing God's good creation, Adam and Eve let sin subdue each of them, through the serpent's lying tongue. The subduers have now been subdued, and the earth that they were supposed to rule over, now strives to rule over them (Gen 3:16–19).

And what will be the solution to the ruin and destruction that Adam and Eve's sin brought into God's good creation? The Lord says to the serpent:

> And I will put enmity between you and the woman, and between your offspring and hers; he will crush your head, and you will strike his heel. (Gen 3:15)

The solution to the failure of Adam and Eve properly to image God, and to subdue the earth, is God's promise to *subdue* Satan, finally and completely, that is, to "crush his head." Even so, Satan will attempt to subdue the offspring of the woman, and in doing so will "strike his heel." Satan's design from Genesis 3 forward has been that he and his followers, instead of the Lord and His people, would subdue the earth.

But their subduing is the antithesis of God's, and thus of God's image. It is a subduing, not to cultivate and promote life, but of murder; a subduing, not to promote and celebrate the truth of God, but of lies (see John 8:42–44). From Genesis 3 to the end of history, the battle between the seed of the serpent and the seed of the woman is a battle of who will subdue whom. This defines the apologetic struggle.

After Adam and Eve sinned, Scripture gives us an account of the first murder. Cain kills his brother Abel. This is the first post-fall example of the hideous kind of subduing, a perversion of the original subduing that was meant to "image" who God is. Cain subdues his brother by murdering him. This is satanic subduing, the direct antithesis of subduing that would image God.

When the Lord comes and speaks to Cain, He tells him that sin wants to subdue him, but that he must subdue it instead (Gen 4:7).

Surely, the Lord is reminding Cain of that original sin of his parents; sin wanted to subdue them, and they should have fulfilled their task to "image" God by subduing their temptation. But they failed. After the fall, the goal of the evil one, and of sin, is to subdue *us*. If we're going to restore even a semblance of God's image in us, we must first find a way to subdue sin.

Cain's sin against God was a perversion of the image of God; it was the antithesis of that image. His murder was certainly a kind of subduing, but it was not subduing "under God"; it was a subduing that was in bondage to the subduing sway of sin. It was, then, an example of the image of God, fallen and twisted.

And so it has been since sin was foisted on the world by our first parents. Since that time, the battle has raged, both in the heavenlies and on earth. It is a battle to the death. It is a battle in which each and every person is engaged, in only one of two ways.

Either a person is subdued by his own sin, and thus acts in ways that are consistent with his "master," or a person dies to himself and is subdued by Christ. There are no other options available to anyone. In each case, we are subdued; we serve one master or the other. Which master we serve ultimately depends on which one subdues us.

In one sense, the history of human beings is the history of subduing. Wars are fought so that one nation can subdue another, or keep from being subdued by another. Medicine is an attempt to subdue the inevitable downward direction of life. Business and industry subdue the earth by creating various products and services in hopes that we will "consume," and thus subdue, what they offer.

Relationships, too, are substantially marked by subduing. An employer subdues his employees in contracting them to work. A group of elders in a church subdue the congregation as they seek to rule over them in a godly way. So also for husbands and wives. These are all examples of how God's character can be "imaged." Since the fall, such "imaging" is marred and distorted.

Many, if not most, crimes are examples of this twisted image, in an urge to subdue. Stealing is subduing what belongs to another; murder is subduing another human being to the point of death. Every kind of abuse has, at root, our "image-urge" to subdue, but it is twisted in opposition to its original intent.

When we consider the image of God in all human beings, then, we should recognize that we all have in common the desire to subdue the earth, in various ways and contexts. If sin had not entered the world, that desire to subdue would "image" God's own character. It would show forth His glory by cultivating what He created, and what He sustains by His providence.

From the smallest molecule to the greatest star, our study of God's creation, and our application of what we learn from it, all demonstrate something of what God is like. Not only so, but human relationships, apart from sin, would exhibit the proper application of subduing, in the home, in our work, and in all our interactions with one another and with God's creation.

It might be a helpful thought experiment to think of all the various aspects of your life and consider to what extent the desire, whether proper or improper, to subdue helps you define and understand what is happening. There is always more to be seen and said, but the image of God, which includes our responsibility to subdue what God has made, remains an important focus of all of life, for every person.

Since the work of Christ has been completed, all authority in heaven and on earth is His. Now that He has ascended, He sits at the Father's right hand—the place of cosmic authority—while His enemies are being subdued and made a footstool for His feet. It is crucial to note—and we will discuss this below—that a central aspect of Christ subduing His enemies was His *humiliation*. That is, subduing can have a subversive element to it; one can subdue by gentleness and respect.

Apologetics and persuasion are both intimately involved in subduing. Because apologetics seeks to defend the Christian faith, it seeks to see people subdued by the grace of Christ. In persuasion, we try to draw people into a Christian context and way of thinking. That "drawing" includes subduing their way of thinking in order to substitute it for the Christian way of thinking. Persuasion hopes to draw people away from their service in the kingdom of darkness in order that the kingdom of light might subdue them, and be the new context for their own efforts to subdue.

If we are drawn to the kingdom of light, we are renewed into the image of Christ. As Christ's image, we can now, by grace, subdue our own sin; we can subdue our errant and wicked thinking; and we can subdue our behavior insofar as it detracts from the glory of God and begin again to show who God is by imaging His character.

When we engage in Christian apologetics with a view to persuasion, we remember that everyone to whom we speak is the image of God. Sin has distorted that image, but it is not destroyed. What we will see in their lives, therefore, are various attempts at subduing.

Their own commitments, their jobs, their hobbies, their interests, will all be different avenues for them to practice subduing. They likely won't see them in that way. But it may be helpful for us to recognize that the image of God drives virtually all of what we do in life, under God. Though sin can seriously pervert and distort that image, the drive to subdue remains in all of us. In apologetics and persuasion, we hope to see the Lord subdue His enemies and draw them to Himself.

IMAGING IMAGES

Our focus in this chapter is on the *person*, the *ethos*, or character of the ones involved in our persuasive apologetic discussions. The section above is basic to that character. The character of every human being is the image of God. It is the responsibility of each and every one of us to live our lives in a way that "images," on a created level, what God is like. Part of that imaging, as we have just seen, includes our desire properly to subdue God's creation.

We subdue God's creation, for example, when we learn more about it. Knowing is a kind of subduing. We subdue when we work to provide a service, or a product, so that life in God's world can be what it was meant to be. There are an almost infinite number of ways that people pursue subduing as we live in God's world.

But we know that life in God's world has been ruined by our sin. When Paul tells us that all have sinned and fallen short of God's glory (Rom 3:23), he is confirming that sin has rendered us incapable of showing—imaging—God's character in the way it was meant to be shown. To fall short of God's glory is to fall short of His image.

As we consider the character of people made in God's image, and the impact of sin on that image, we need to look at Paul's discussion of these matters in the first chapter of Romans. If we were going to identify a "hub" out of which all the spokes project to form the "wheel" of apologetics and persuasion, Paul's teaching in the last half of this chapter would be that hub.

The book of Romans has been a highly influential book in the history of the church. Augustine, Martin Luther, Charles Wesley, and others acknowledge its influence in their own lives and ministries.

One of the reasons for that influence is that, as Paul writes this epistle to this important location, he has yet to visit them (Rom 1:10–13). Since he has not yet visited them, one of his chief concerns is to explain to them the wonder of the gospel in all of its multifaceted depth and richness. He tells them that he is not ashamed of the gospel, and it is that gospel that has the power to save (1:16).

As he begins to explain to them just what that gospel is, he begins, not with the good news of the gospel, but with the bad news of our sinfulness. We don't really understand the good news of the gospel unless we first recognize the bad news of our sin against God. (This would be another place where it would help you to have your Bible open as we think together about Scripture's teaching in this chapter.)

Beginning in verse 18, Scripture describes the condition of all human beings since our fall into sin. Not only that, but it tells us about God's own disposition with respect to our sin. So, he says:

The wrath of God is being revealed from heaven against all the god-
lessness and wickedness of people, who suppress the truth by their
wickedness, since what may be known about God is plain to them,
because God has made it plain to them. (Rom 1:18–19)

There is a mountain of rich, biblical truth in these two verses. First,
we are to understand that God's displeasure toward our sin is being
revealed from heaven. We won't be able to look closely at the effects of
God's wrath in this chapter, but it would be useful to see how Scripture
elaborates on the reality of our sinful progression as an expression of
God's wrath in verses 26–32.

The reason that God's wrath is revealed from heaven is that we, by
our wickedness, suppress the truth. As Paul writes under the inspiration
of the Holy Spirit, he recognizes that he has introduced two ideas in this
verse that will need some explanation. The first idea is "suppress" and the
second is "truth." He explains the second one first.

What could Paul mean by "truth" in verse 18? Since the passage is
meant to apply to all people everywhere, what "truth" do all people have,
but suppress? Surely, he would not at this point be referring to the truth
of the gospel of Jesus Christ. He has not yet explained that truth (he will
begin to do that in earnest in chapter 3). And it is common knowledge
that not every person has yet heard the truth of the gospel. So, what is
this "truth" that we all have but suppress?

Verse 19 begins to answer that question. The truth that is suppressed,
says Paul, is "what may be known about God." Now we see that there is
some kind of universal truth that includes what may be known about
God. We also see that "what may be known about God" is "plain" to us.
It is plain to us "because God has made it plain" to us.

So, we see two important aspects to this truth that all people have
—(1) It is truth about God, that is, "what may be known" about Him,
and (2) God is the one who makes what may be known about Him
"plain" to us. With this in mind, Paul can get a little more specific
(1:20):

For since the creation of the world God's invisible qualities—his eternal power and divine nature—have been clearly seen, being understood from what has been made, so that people are without excuse.

Now we see that "what may be known about God" includes "his eternal power and divine nature." These two categories are intentionally broad. They are meant to include both what God *does* (eternal power), as well as who God *is* (divine nature). In that sense, they are all-inclusive of God's character as God; they include His character and His power.

Paul is not interested in spelling out exactly, in every detail, what each person knows and when. That kind of focus would detract from his central point. His central point is that all people know the true God *truly*. We know the true God truly "because God has made it plain" to us.

And we see in verse 20 that the means that God uses to make Himself known to each and every one of us is "what has been made." The theological category that Paul gives us here is commonly called God's "natural revelation." The adjective itself may not be as clear as it could be; the word "natural" can mean a number of things. Specifically, Paul is telling us that God is known *in and through His creation.* That is what is meant by "natural" in natural revelation; it is "creational" revelation.

Whatever the specific content of the knowledge that each of us has, Paul makes clear that it is sufficient to render all of us "without excuse" before God. In other words, since God is the one who "makes it plain" to us, He ensures, by revealing Himself constantly in and through all of creation, that we have true knowledge of Him so that our sin against Him is inexcusable. No one, in other words, will stand before God's judgment throne and say, "I didn't know you." God has made His revelation of Himself plain through what He has made.

We should be clear here that the knowledge that we have through God's revelation in creation is *not* the knowledge of the gospel, or of Christ and what He has done. The two categories Paul uses—"eternal power and divine nature"—refer us to the attributes and power of God, power which we recognize as "eternal." That is, when we live and move in God's world, God makes plain who He is and that He is the one sustaining and maintaining His creation through His transcendent (eternal) power.

To this point, Paul has fleshed out what he means by "truth" in verse 18. The truth is the knowledge of God that all people have, because God makes it plain in us through what He has made. It is knowledge sufficient to condemn us if we refuse to bow the knee in faith and acknowledge it. And, as it turns out, when we remain in our sins, that is exactly what we do.

The second idea that Paul brings up in verse 18 is "suppress." This notion is consistent with our previous discussion of "subduing." God plainly makes Himself known to us in and through creation. But, instead of acknowledging what we know, instead of accepting that knowledge as our own, we attempt to "suppress" or "subdue" it. Instead of being subdued by the truth that God gives to us, so that we honor Him as God and give Him thanks (v. 21), we try to hold the truth down. What does this suppression look like?

> For although they knew God, they neither glorified him as God nor gave thanks to him, but their thinking became futile and their foolish hearts were darkened. Although they claimed to be wise, they became fools and exchanged the glory of the immortal God for images made to look like a mortal human being and birds and animals and reptiles. They exchanged the truth about God for a lie, and worshiped and served created things rather than the Creator—who is forever praised. Amen. (1:21–23, 25)

Paul is explaining to us what our sin looks like, even as we remain the image of God. He has in view the condition of all people *after* the fall. Notice that, in suppressing the truth that God makes plain to us, we exchange "the glory of the immortal God for images . . ." As those who have fallen short of the glory of God because of our sin, we exchange that glory, which is His image in us, for created images.

As Paul writes these words, he clearly has the creation account from Genesis 1 and 2 in mind. The list of images that we prefer to worship, as we seek to exchange the glory of God, moves backward from the actual order of creation in Genesis—from mortal man (Gen 1:26) to birds (Gen 1:20) to animals and reptiles (Gen 1:24). The point Paul is making is that the image of God, as originally created, is now distorted by sin to such an extent that it seeks to move inexorably *away* from the God who created everything (and who we're meant to image) and *toward* created things. In other words, it is a sinful regress instead of human progress.

Paul explains this exchange in another, though similar, way in verse 25. There he says we exchange "the truth about God for a lie." Here again he is clearly referring us to that first, fatal sin. When Adam and Eve were in the garden being tempted by Satan, they took God's own words—the truth of God—and exchanged them for Satan's lies: "You will not die." That exchange, Paul makes clear, involves the worship and service of created things, rather than the Creator.

In other words, our suppression of the truth means that, instead of imaging God and showing His glory, we seek to *image images*. We take what God has made and exalt those things to the status of gods. Instead of being properly subdued by God's image in us, so that we subdue the earth *under Him*, we subdue the knowledge of Him that He continues to give to us and allow created things to subdue *us*; we "worship and *serve*" them. This is the perversion of the image of God in all of us, since the fall.

So, there is good news and bad news with respect to our character as sinners who are made in God's image. The good news is that there is no person alive (who is self-conscious) who is not at the same time God-conscious. Everyone, because we remain in the image of God, *knows* God. We will see in the next chapter how Paul applies these truths to his audience in seeking to defend Christianity and to persuade them.

The bad news is that, even though we know God, we are loathe to acknowledge what we know. Instead, because of our sin, we seek to subdue and bury the knowledge that God continues to give us. We substitute idols for the true God. We find or make created things to worship and serve so that we won't have to bow the knee to the God whom we know. We pervert the goodness of the image of God. In doing so, we pervert our own behavior and thinking (Rom 1:24).

In thinking about apologetics and persuasion, the fact that all people know God is central and vital for our task. Even though we, in our sin, seek to subdue the clear and plain knowledge that God gives to us, we can no more eradicate that knowledge than we can eradicate our own existence. It is because we remain in God's image that He ensures we will know Him. We will always know the One we're meant to image.

In knowing Him, our response *should be* to "image" Him, to glorify Him and enjoy Him forever. But our sin tries to build an impenetrable wall between our knowledge of God and our own perverse desires. It sets in the foreground all of those created things that delight and please us—things to which we will entrust our very lives—even as it continually pushes down that knowledge of God that He "makes plain" to us.

In our apologetics and in persuasion, the fact that all people to whom we defend the faith actually know Him is a monumental truth that should set the tone for our persuasive communication to others. Every person to whom we speak is a person who truly knows the God of whom we speak. The goal of persuasion is to see how that knowledge is "lived out" in those to whom we speak. I will go into this more later.

This knowledge likely won't be admitted by them; that's what suppression of the truth does. But suppression of the truth assumes *the truth*. If there is no truth, there is nothing to suppress. So, it is that truth, the knowledge of God that God gives and makes plain, that is a central component of our appeal when we engage in apologetics and persuasion.

We saw in chapter 1 that God's speech to us is His initial "bridge" that connects human beings to Him. As with God's speech, this universal knowledge of Him that bombards each of us through all that He has made is a "bridge" that *God* builds between those who are in Christ and those who oppose Him. The God that Christians know and love is the same God that those who are apart from Christ also know. We will return to this in the next chapter.

PATRONAGE OF VICES

So far, what have we learned about our *ethos*? We have learned two universal aspects of what it means to be human. First, we see that each person is meant to "image" God. That is why we were put on the earth. In the words of the *Westminster Shorter Catechism*, our purpose on this earth is to "glorify God and enjoy Him forever." This is true, not just for Christians, but for every human being. So, the universal human *ethos* is meant to be God-directed, not man-directed. Every human creature should be focused on God and His character.

But we have also learned that, sadly, because of the effects of sin, we try to focus on anything but God. We do this, however, with the full realization of who God is and of our dependence on Him. We *know* the One we're supposed to image. We are not ignorant of His character. We suppress it, to be sure, but we continue to know what we suppress. These two intertwined truths—the image of God and the knowledge of God—are the universal *ethos* of every person. This is who we are as human beings.

There is one more centrally important aspect to our character as human beings, our *ethos*, that will help us think about how we might persuasively defend the faith. As we have seen, Scripture is clear that in and through natural revelation, we all, since we are images of God, know the true God truly.

But this knowledge that we all have is not something that just flutters in the mind. It is not an abstraction, or a mere fact, that we have locked up in our brains. Instead, Paul goes on to assert that this knowledge has *ethical* or *moral* truths embedded in it. To know God is to know what

He requires of us. So, says Paul, with respect to our universal knowledge of God:

> Although they know God's righteous decree that those who do such things deserve death, they not only continue to do these very things but also approve of those who practice them. (Rom 1:32)

This is a fascinating truth that the Lord reveals to us through His apostle. It is designed, in part, to assure us that the universal knowledge of God that all people have carries with it a basic and true knowledge of right and wrong.

The word that Paul uses in this verse, translated as "righteous decree" is explained for us in Romans 2:14–15. There he says:

> (Indeed, when Gentiles, who do not have the law, do by nature things required by the law, they are a law for themselves, even though they do not have the law. They show that the requirements of the law are written on their hearts, their consciences also bearing witness, and their thoughts sometimes accusing them and at other times even defending them.)

In other words, even though the Jews had the law given to them through Moses, we should not think that the Gentiles were given no knowledge of the law at all. Instead, Scripture describes for us Gentiles doing "by nature" things required by the law. How could that be? How could Gentiles, who were not given a written law, recognize the sin of idolatry, or seek not to lie, or steal or murder? How could they recognize the basic value of property, of truth, or of human life?

The answer, says Paul, is *again* in what *God does* in the human heart. As people live and breathe in God's world, and thus know the God who made them, they also "have the requirements of the law" written on their hearts by God Himself, in and through all that He has made (including within them!). That is, as God makes Himself known in and through creation, He also makes known to every person His requirements so that they know what it means to live according to God's standard and character.

As Scripture goes on to note, however, instead of acknowledging that those requirements are God-given and God-revealing, we, in our sins, continue not only to oppose them, but also to cheer on others who oppose them. This, too, is evidence of the *suppression* of the truth, rather than *ignorance* of it. We break God's requirements, Scripture says, even though we recognize that our transgressions are worthy of death.

We need to take seriously this substantial reality within all people. As with our knowledge of God, which we suppress and exchange, so also with the moral requirements of God's law. We suppress those requirements in that we, in our sins, will not give God His due in our lives. Instead of living according to His requirements and His law, which He Himself has made known to all, we hold those things down and attempt to live according to what *we* want; we make our own laws. We seek to be, literally, *autonomous*, ruled by the laws we create, rather than God's law.

In a well-known letter to a public newspaper, the atheist British philosopher Bertrand Russell wrote about the notion that morality was likely a matter of personal taste. He knew, however, that such a view was completely untenable. Was the Reich of Hitler merely a matter of personal taste? The regime of Pol Pot? The latest murder in the city? The abuse of children? Are these no different than my preference for roast rather than ham? Russell knew this view could not be sustained. He had to finally concede, "I cannot live as though ethical values were simply a matter of personal taste. I do not know the solution to this."[2]

The "solution" that Russell would not concede is the knowledge of God, and of His requirements, that God implants in us all. With that knowledge, we recognize that morality comes to us from the outside, in. It is *not* a matter of personal taste, but is instead a revelation of God's own

2. *The Observer*, October 6, 1957.

character, given to us in and through our consciences. It has its firm roots and foundation, not in what I would *prefer*, but in who God is. No more solid foundation could be had than this.

But, this passage in Scripture teaches us that our suppression of this "moral" truth leads us to encourage the chaos of sin both in ourselves and in others, rather than acknowledge the goodness of God's own character. Our sin moves us to prefer chaos—Russell's "no solution"—rather than recognize the firm foundation of God's character. John Calvin, in his comment on Romans 1:32, put it this way:

> . . . when such an impudence is contracted through a sinful habit, that vices, and not virtues, please us, and are approved, there is no more any hope of reformation. Such, then, is the interpretation I give; for I see that the Apostle meant here to condemn something more grievous and more wicked than the very doing of vices . . . ,—that is, when wretched men, having cast away all shame, undertake the patronage of vices in opposition to the righteousness of God.[3]

Calvin's point is that when we see around us a deluge of sinful behavior in society, we should view that as a kind of "group think," where an entire group is suppressing the knowledge of God in much the same way. We should see in such behavior the "patronage of vices," that is, a majority opinion that what is wrong, is right, and what is right, is wrong. This is suppression writ large on society. It has its origin, not in ignorance, but in the *suppressed* knowledge of God and His requirements. It is a concerted effort to cover sin up, and to excuse it by affirming it as normal for us and for everyone around us.

We may begin to see, however, that such knowledge can function as an aspect of our persuasive apologetic. Knowing from Scripture that all people know God truly, *including* the fact that we know what God

---

3. John Calvin and John Owen, *Commentary on the Epistle of Paul the Apostle to the Romans* (Bellingham, WA: Logos Bible Software, 2010), 83.

requires of us, can help us assess points of persuasion in those to whom we speak. We'll examine that more in the following chapters.

THE CHRISTIAN *ETHOS*: GENTLENESS AND RESPECT

There are two universal truths that we have just noted with respect to human beings. The first is that we all remain the image of God. That image is tarnished; it is distorted and twisted in multiple ways. We have fallen short of that image. Instead of imaging God, we seek to image images. We are, in our sins, idolaters. As John Calvin puts it, our hearts are "idol factories."[4] But the *fact* that we still choose to worship something, even if an idol, suggests that we recognize the importance of worshiping and serving something beyond us.

This is evidence of our second universal truth. Because we are His image, all people know God. We know Him because He makes Himself known. He reveals Himself to us each and every minute of each and every day. That revelation gets through to us.

But if we remain in our sins, we suppress, subdue, or hold down that knowledge. We would rather worship and serve an image, something in creation, than worship and serve the true God. In knowing God, we know what He requires of us. That, too, we suppress and exchange. These two truths are central to the character of anyone to whom we speak. God has made us in His image. As His image, we know the God we're meant to image.

Given these two universal truths of human character (*ethos*), we move now from what we all have in common, as human beings made in God's image, to the division between those who are in Christ and those who remain in slavery to their sins (Rom 6:19–20). Because of that division,

4. John Calvin and Henry Beveridge, *Commentary upon the Acts of the Apostles*, vol. 2 (Bellingham, WA: Logos Bible Software, 2010), 413.

there is a need for defending Christianity, and for seeking to defend persuasively.

We now turn our attention more specifically to the apologetic task that is the privilege of every Christian. Included in that task is the *character*, the *ethos*, of the one(s) who are given the privilege of persuasively defending Christianity.

In the apostle Peter's first epistle, he is concerned to encourage suffering Christians to persevere in their faith, even amid the trials that have come their way. His initial audience consisted of scattered exiles (1 Pet 1:1) who have "had to suffer grief in all kinds of trials" (1 Pet 1:6). In these trials, Peter encourages them to be holy because God is holy (1:16) and to live their lives in "reverent fear" (1:17; 2:17–18).

As they are encouraged to be holy amid suffering, Peter also tells them how to respond to those who are against them:

> But in your hearts revere Christ as Lord. Always be prepared to give an answer to everyone who asks you to give the reason for the hope that you have. But do this with gentleness and respect. (1 Pet 3:15)

The first thing that Christians must do is ensure that the universal Lordship of Christ is a settled matter in their own hearts. This is crucial, especially amid suffering. We are to recognize that no suffering comes to us unless the Lord of heaven and earth ordains it. Our suffering is never an evidence that the sovereign purposes of Christ are thwarted. Instead, we are called to suffer, *because Christ suffered for us*, leaving us an example so that we would follow in His steps (1 Pet 2:21).

In that way, our suffering is meant to be an *example* of Christ's Lordship, not evidence against it. Because Jesus suffered, He now sits at God's right hand and is subduing His enemies. So also, when we set Christ apart as Lord in our hearts, we see our suffering as evidence that He reigns and that we are His. Our suffering is linked to His, our humiliation to His humiliation.

In our defense of Christianity, when we believe in our hearts that

Christ is Lord, we see the attacks and objections that come against Christ and His truth for what they are. They are *not* attacks that threaten Christ's Lordship; nothing can remove him from His Father's right hand. Neither are there objections that could actually turn the truth of Christ's word into lies. As we have seen, when He speaks, He speaks nothing but the truth. That truth remains our foundation, even if objections and attacks inundate us.

Once the Lordship of Christ is planted deeply in our hearts so that there is no possibility of uprooting it, Peter tells us to "always be prepared to give an answer." The Greek word translated "to give an answer" is the word *apologia*. It is the word from which we get the English word "apologetics." Peter is telling his readers, then and now, that part of our Christian responsibility in this world is to prepare ourselves to defend the Christian faith.

We shouldn't pass too quickly from this truth. We should recognize here that the Bible is placing the responsibility to do apologetics squarely on the shoulders of Christ's sheep, His people. It is the church that is given the privilege of defending the honor of her Savior.

It may be that this emphasis has been lost in discussions about apologetics. Many still may believe that apologetics is meant for the "professional," the "academic," the "skilled debater." No doubt, academics and skilled debaters can be very useful in defending Christianity. There are people who are particularly adept at thinking through the truths of Scripture and their implications for unbelief.

But Peter's point is that all of us who are in Christ are invited into the privilege of "giving an answer." As those who follow Christ, we are meant to be "always ready" when questions, concerns, or objections might come our way. And if we are all meant to do apologetics, we can be assured that the Lord has given us the resources to accomplish that task. He would not call His sheep to do something without providing the resources needed to accomplish what He asks us to do.

This brings us back to the subject matter of the previous chapter. The reason that we are all able to engage in the apologetic task is that the

Lord has given us the sufficient means to defend Him. Those means are His Word and His Spirit.

His Word is necessary because in order to defend the faith, we need God's own truth. As we have seen, the Lord's people have always had His revealed truth, both through creation and in His spoken/written word. His Spirit is necessary because, as we saw in the last chapter, without the Spirit speaking by and with the Word, we cannot be fully persuaded of the truth of the gospel.

If we recognize the original audience to whom Peter wrote, it might help us see this better. These were a scattered group of Christian believers. We cannot assume that they were all professional debaters or skilled academics. Likely, they were Christians who were suffering because of their commitment to Christ.

It was that suffering, perhaps, that would give them a proper perspective on their "hope" in Christ. It was their current condition as a persecuted church that would focus their attention on the reality of their life after death. It may have even been that their suffering made them *better* apologists.

The biblical point, however, is that all of God's people are equipped to defend the faith He has graciously given to them. We are all equipped because we all recognize the truth of what God has spoken in His Word. Included in that truth is the fact that, because of sin, suffering is universal. But it is not final for those who trust in Christ.

Once we recognize the unalterable and universal Lordship of Christ and set that truth firmly within our hearts, because we have His Word and His Spirit, we need not fear the objections and attacks that might come against Him. Instead, we can see all of them, as we see our suffering, as evidence of Christ's sovereign rule over His creation. Attacks and objections are means that the Lord uses to bring people to Himself. This is why our defense in the face of such attacks is so important.

We are to be "always ready" to defend the truth of our Lord and Savior. More specifically, Peter says we are to be ready to defend the faith "to everyone who asks you to give the reason for the hope that you have."

The word translated "reason" in this verse is a word we've seen before; it is the Greek word *logos*. That word has a range of translation possibilities. It is properly translated "reason" in this verse, but it also carries with it the notion of "word" or even "logic."

The point Peter is making is that, in our defense of Christianity, we need to be prepared to offer a *word* of hope, or to explain the *logic* or rationale for our hope in Christ. In the context of Peter's original audience, this was a key point. It is a key point for us as well. Even in suffering— perhaps *especially* in suffering—we should be able to explain to those who are outside of Christ why it is that we still have *hope*.

From the perspective of those outside of Christ, whatever hope there might be is a hope without any real content. Even though it is commonplace to conclude that anyone who dies goes to "a better place," there is no real reason to think so unless we understand why there is death in the first place.

What hope is there for those who are apart from Christ? How can suffering be meaningful in any way if the end of it all is destruction (Phil 3:19; 2 Thess 1:9; 2 Pet 2:1; 3:7, 12, 16)? Our defense of Christianity should include a persuasive reason for our hope in Christ.

As Scripture makes clear, "Sin entered the world through one man, and death through sin" (Rom 5:12). The reason for suffering and for death, therefore, is that sin, through one man, intruded into God's good creation and brought ruin. The fundamental problem in all of creation is sin's sometimes overwhelming influence in it. The entire creation groans because of this influence (Rom 8:22). And we, as sinners, participate in this influence and perpetuate it.

Apart from this truth, death is seen as just a "natural" part of everyday life. It is what happens to everyone, without discrimination. It's just the way the world is. And, if that is true, then it becomes difficult to find a foundation for real hope. If death is the way the world is, then how could we *know* that something blissful or blessed beyond death awaits us? We might hope for such a thing, but our hope would be empty. There would be no *reason* for it, no real content to it. It would be hope in hope, which is futile.

The *reason* for the hope that Christians have is that Christ has conquered sin and death on the cross. Since death comes through sin, only the subduing and destruction of sin can ultimately subdue death itself. So, we can have hope as creation groans, as we suffer, as we see death all around us, because we know the one who was victorious over death, over sin, and over suffering. Without Christ and what He has accomplished, there is no hope available to us, or to anyone.

Peter's final command moves us to a particular focus on our own character—the *ethos* of persuasion—as we prepare ourselves to give an answer. Peter says we are to give our answers "with gentleness and respect."

The word used for "gentleness" here could also be translated "meekness." In order to understand the word properly, it may help to know that this word is used only one more time in the New Testament. It is a word that Jesus uses to describe Himself.

In Matthew 11:28–30, as Jesus turns His attention to the crowd around Him, He calls them to come to Him:

> Come to me, all you who are weary and burdened, and I will give you rest. Take my yoke upon you and learn from me, for I am gentle and humble in heart, and you will find rest for your souls. For my yoke is easy and my burden is light.

Notice the compassion of the Savior as He appeals to the crowd. He knows that our sin can be a burden to us, that it can make us weary. So He promises rest to those who recognize their burden and who come to Him.

As He summons the crowd, He also wants them to see that those who would come to Him would also take up His yoke. That might initially sound like trading in one burden for another. But Jesus wants the crowd to know what kind of person He is, so that they might properly understand what kind of yoke they would take upon them. It is true, as we have seen, that moving from slavery to sin to serving Christ is a movement from one master to another. But, with Christ as our master, we move to One who is not cruel and unrelenting.

Instead, Jesus describes Himself as "gentle and humble in heart." The word "gentle" here is the same one Peter uses above. Surely, Peter would have remembered these words from his Savior on that day. As Jesus Himself was subject to attacks and objections to his teaching, Peter would have recognized the gentleness and humility of Christ toward his accusers.

What, exactly, is this gentleness that characterizes Jesus and is supposed to characterize us as we respond to objections? Just prior to these words of Jesus in Matthew 11, we see Him pronouncing "woes" on the various cities that He had visited because of their failure to repent (Matt 11:20–24). Those "woes" may not sound like they come from one who is "gentle." If we properly understand gentleness, however, we can see how those woes can be gentle.

The gentleness of Jesus includes the recognition that repentance is an "easy yoke" compared to the stubborn refusal to come to Him. The reason, in other words, that Jesus is pronouncing woes on the cities that rejected Him is because of His compassion on those cities. He knew that they remained "weary and burdened" because, even though they saw His great works, they refused to come to Him.

The gentleness that characterizes Jesus, and that should characterize our defense of Christianity, is something like a "calm confidence" in the truth of God and in His sovereign ability to work His will in the world, even among His enemies. As a matter of fact, just before Jesus turns to call the crowd to come to Him, He prays to His Father:

> At that time Jesus said, "I praise you, Father, Lord of heaven and earth, because you have hidden these things from the wise and learned, and revealed them to little children. Yes, Father, for this was your good pleasure. (Matt 11:25–26 [NIV 1984])

Jesus is gentle, in part, because He knows that the objections and attacks that He has received and endured are all a part of His Father's sovereign plan. As a matter of fact, Jesus *praises* His Father for the fact that those who consider themselves wise and learned are, in fact, hidden from the reality of who Christ is.

This truth should motivate gentleness in us as well when questions or objections or attacks come our way. *Whatever* comes our way is part of the Father's sovereign plan for His world, and it serves, in the end, to glorify and honor Him for who He is.

We can be gentle in our apologetic because we know that we are not in control of anything, in the end. We are not in control of the objections and attacks that come, and we are not in control of how our answers will be received. We are not in control of those to whom we speak. We are not in control of the salvation that comes through the communication of the gospel. We can be instruments the Lord will use, but we cannot be in charge of what the Lord will determine to do.

When questions come, or objections are raised, we can have a "calm confidence" because we know that our heavenly Father is perfectly orchestrating every word, every conversation, every person, at all times, in order to accomplish His perfect plan. And if we are confident in our Father and His plan, we have no reason to be agitated or angry toward our questioners and accusers.

We should also notice the persuasive character of this "gentleness." As Jesus calls the crowd, He appeals to those who know that they are "weary and burdened." And what is something that those who know they are weary would surely want? Rest!

The rest that Jesus promises can motivate those who know of their burden to come to Him. It is, as a matter of fact, the one key thing that those who are weary and burdened know they need. The rest that Jesus promises, the yoke that is "easy" and "light," are all a part of the gentleness of Jesus. He is not an unjust taskmaster who places undue pressures and burdens on people. Sin does that, but Jesus does not.

Our gentleness is an avenue of persuasion as we respond to questions and objections. We want people to know the rest that Jesus provides. If we become agitated, or angry, or impatient, or irritated with those who question us, we will mirror those whose taskmaster is burdensome. We will give the impression that our task is up to us, that it is done in our own strength (or lack thereof). We will not model those who are supposed to be at rest, trusting our Savior as we listen and speak.

We can be gentle because we know that true rest and gentleness is found not in us or in our own efforts. True rest and gentleness is found in Christ alone. And His heavenly Father, and ours, is working all things, even our conversations, for His own glory. This is the crux of a Christian *ethos*.

In answering those who would come with questions, then, we are to image the one who is gentle and humble in heart. We are to be gentle in heart, even as He is gentle in heart. Our gentleness is exactly what those who live with the harshness of their own sin need. It is a characteristic of persuasion; it should be a gentleness that draws people *from* themselves and *to* Christ.

Peter says we are to respond to people "with gentleness and respect." The word for "respect" here is the Greek word *phobos*. It is the word that we use oftentimes for various "phobias," or fears. While it could mean "respect," it can also mean here "reverence" or "fear."

Given the context of Peter's discussion here, it is plausible, maybe even likely, that *phobos* is referring to the fear of God that should accompany our persuasive and apologetic responses. As Peter begins this discussion on apologetics, he quotes from Isaiah 8:12. He says in 1 Peter 3:14:

> But even if you should suffer for what is right, you are blessed. "Do not fear their threats; do not be frightened."

So, initially, we are not to fear the threats of others, or to be frightened.

Though Peter uses this verse to encourage us to "set apart Christ as Lord," the next verse in Isaiah says this:

> The LORD Almighty is the one you are to regard as holy, he is the one you are to fear, he is the one you are to dread . . . (Isa 8:13)

The original audience to whom Peter writes would have recognized the connection between Isaiah 8:13 and Peter's own words to them here.

They would have known that Peter's admonition that we "set apart Christ as holy" was in significant ways identical to Isaiah's summons to fear the Lord.

The point that Peter wants to make when he encourages us to respond with "gentleness and respect" is that our respect, our reverence, our fear, is to be directed, not, in the first place, toward those to whom we speak, but to the Lord Himself.

In other words, we engage with unbelief with a full recognition that the Lord of heaven and earth is the Judge of heaven and earth. And while we recognize that our judgment is secured in Christ, so that we will not be found guilty before Him, we also recognize that those to whom we speak live their lives under the terrible judgment of the One who now reigns in heaven.

In keeping with one of our emphases thus far, we could say that Peter is encouraging us to recognize, as we speak to others, that the Lord who is holy and who sits on His throne will one day judge the ones to whom we speak. That judgment is a terrifying judgment; it is a judgment of fear and of dread.

In Christ, we see that the fear and dread of our judgment is removed, since it was placed on Him at the cross. But it is not removed from those who object to Christ, or who attack His truth. And so, we defend the faith with the firm recognition that Christ will come as judge, and that His judgment will be terrible for those found without faith in Him.

The character of the Christian apologist, therefore, is marked by gentleness toward those to whom we speak and the proper fear of the Lord in His holiness. These characteristics should instill in us a "calm confidence" as we respond to questions, and it should keep our eyes looking up, where Christ is seated at the right hand of God. The Christian ethos of persuasion is an ethos of trust and faith in Christ throughout our discussions. We trust Him, and we properly fear Him. Our primary focus, in other words, in our persuasive apologetic discussions is not on our opponents or on the objections given. Our focus is set on Christ Himself.

CHRISTIAN CHARACTER

Now we can begin to see the importance of the armor from Ephesians 6 that we discussed previously. Let's see the list again as we think about our own character, our *ethos*, as persuasive apologists. We are to put on:

- the belt of truth buckled around your waist,
- the breastplate of righteousness
- your feet fitted with the readiness that comes from the gospel of peace
- the shield of faith, with which you can extinguish all the flaming arrows of the evil one
- the helmet of salvation (Eph 6:14–17).

All this armor refers us to our character (*ethos*) as Christians. The belt of truth requires us to view God's world as He has described it in His Word. The breastplate of righteousness is demonstrated in our desire to please and obey our Savior. Our feet show our readiness to bring "the gospel of peace" to those who are at war against Christ. The shield of faith is worn so that we never lose sight of the fact that Christ is on His throne, and He reigns no matter what is happening as we speak to others. Our helmet of salvation, in a sense, protects our minds from thinking that anything that we do, or that others must do, is wholly within their grasp. Salvation is from the Lord, and our helmet constantly reminds us of that great truth.

In the end, the armor that we don is "character" armor. It is central to the *ethos* of our persuasive apologetic. It is a visible manifestation of the words that we speak as we engage others with the truth of God's Word. It is what motivates our gentleness and fear.

Os Guinness suggests that, second only to the problem of evil, is the problem of hypocrisy.[5] He may be correct. For that reason, the *ethos*

---

5. Os Guinness, *Fool's Talk: Recovering the Art of Christian Persuasion* (InterVarsity Press, Kindle Edition), loc. 3206.

of apologetics and persuasion is vitally important if we want our audience to take our words as seriously as they ought. We may have uncanny insight into the context and situation of those to whom we speak, and we may be utterly eloquent in our communication of the truth of God's Word, but if our character (*ethos*) speaks against the truth that we hope to communicate, we will have spoken in vain. Of course, the Lord can use any communication of His truth to bring people to Himself. Our responsibility, however, is to don the Lord's armor and to respond with gentleness and the fear of the Lord.

We are to be careful to "match" our behavior with the truth we speak. This does not at all mean we need to be perfect. Instead, it means that we can admit our inability to follow Christ perfectly, even as we show our real desire to be His disciples. The *ethos* of the Christian is that we are imperfect, sinful people who long each day to follow Christ more and more. We embrace the privilege of taking up our cross daily and following Him.

There is one more concluding, critical point to note as we think about our own character—our *ethos*—as those who desire to defend Christianity and to persuade. The point is this: the *ethos* of the person must be measured not by those to whom we speak. It must be measured, in the first place, by the Word of God.

This is an important point because it recognizes that the *standard* for our character is not to be determined by others but can only be given to us in Scripture. We will remember, for example, that on one occasion the Jews accused Jesus of being demon-possessed (John 8:48). Surely, this accusation was as far from reality as it could possibly be. They judged Jesus's character to be evil, when they were confronted with the only one who was without any sin whatsoever.

As we will see in the next chapter, when Paul was in the marketplace in Athens, some who were listening to him called him a "babbler" (Acts 17:18). They judged Paul's character to be so deficient that he was unable to make sense of anything he was saying. But those kinds of judgments are not what count as our *ethos*.

In each of these cases, the standard for judging the *ethos* of the one speaking was the wrong standard. Jesus and Paul were both being judged by errant, human standards and were found deficient in character based on those standards. But there was, in fact, no deficiency at all.

When we seek to be people of Christian character, therefore, we remember that such character can only be properly measured by the standard of the Word of God. In His Word, we have all that we need to see ourselves properly, and, by the grace of God, to adjust our character as we pursue sanctification in this life. Our concern for *ethos*, therefore, is not a concern to please our audience, in the first place, but is a concern to please the Lord as we speak apologetically and persuasively about the Christian faith.

With respect to the character that is important in our persuasive defense of Christianity, therefore, we have both a universal *ethos*, and then, based on that *ethos*, a specifically Christian *ethos*. Universally, all people are and remain the image of God. Apart from Christ, that image is marred and distorted, but it nevertheless defines who we are as God's human creatures. Included in the image of God is the universal knowledge of God that all people have, including the knowledge of what He requires of us all. The Lord has never left Himself without a witness to who He is (Acts 14:17). Being the image of God means knowing Him, and knowing that we are responsible to glorify Him, that is, to demonstrate by our lives what He is like.

More specifically, though, those who are in Christ are being renewed more and more into His image. That image includes knowledge, righteousness, and holiness (Col 3:10; Eph 4:24). Our renewed knowledge is now centered around God's own revelation, in creation and in His Word. Christians know Him according to what He has said in Scripture, and we long for others to know Him as well. Our renewed righteousness and holiness include our passion to be more and more like Christ. We delight to do His will as we recognize our own process of sanctification. Like Him, we want to be gentle and offer burdened people the only rest that can satisfy them—the rest that Christ Himself promises to give.

So, we fully arm ourselves for the battle. The battle is the Lord's, so we wear the very armor that He Himself wore. We engage the battle with Him as the Divine Warrior. We engage the battle, as He did, with gentleness and fear, because we know that the battle is best fought when it is fought by those who follow their Leader.

FIVE

PATHOS

In this chapter, we move from that first crucial component of persuasion, *ethos*, to the second one, *pathos*. *Pathos* could refer to a number of things. In this context, it points us to our audience. The word "pathos" is part of our English words "sym*pathy*" and "em*pathy*." Both of those words are "other" directed. They indicate that we are putting ourselves, as it were, in the "skin" of someone else, so that we might better relate to their particular plight or circumstance.

Whenever we consider how to persuade those to whom we speak, it is important, as far as possible, to understand as much as we can about those who are listening to us. In the words of Aristotle from the previous chapter, it means "putting the audience into a certain frame of mind." We can only do that as we consider what the audience's "frame of mind" currently *is*. That "certain frame of mind" is one that might draw them into the truth that we present, rather than push them away from it.

In the example I gave in the introduction, I was diligent to tell my friend all that he needed to know about the gospel: God's work in creating us, our fall into sin, his own sin, the cross, the resurrection of Christ, and our responsibility to believe. What I had *not* considered in all of my discussion was *pathos*. I had not taken the time to ask him about his particular sense of need, or his own circumstances, or his own reaction to the truths I was communicating. My sole concern was the truth; I had not even thought of presenting the truth persuasively.

This brings me to a point that I have only slowly recognized. One of the best ways to recognize the importance of *pathos* in apologetics is to listen well enough so that more questions can be asked. When I was commending those great gospel truths to my friend, that's *all* I was doing. I was telling him those truths.

The Lord can certainly use those truths according to their power and His sovereignty. But I was not at all concerned to ask him about himself, or his reactions to what I was saying, or to see where he thought he was in his own life at that point. Asking good questions is an art for most of us; it needs to be practiced over and over again. But being aware of its importance is half the battle. It shows that our concern is not simply an "abstract" concern about truth, but that our concern is *personal*. We want to be able to sym*pathize* and em*pathize* with their own situations and circumstances as much as we can.

God expresses his incomprehensible character in a way that we can understand. We know God because he reveals himself anthropomorphically. We saw in chapter 1 that the Lord connected to Adam and Eve through *words*. Those words were the means He used to establish the relationship He had made with them. They reveal who He is and what He requires.

That is, by *connecting* to us with human words, the Lord reveals Himself *persuasively*. Since one important aspect of persuasion is connection, in condescension God is connecting Himself with His human creatures in ways, or modes, which He Himself created and which those creatures can understand. We understand God's words because He made us to be receivers of, and responders to, human speech.

The quintessential "connection" between us and God, as we have seen, is in the Word Himself, the Lord Jesus Christ. In Christ, God does not simply tell us about Himself; He becomes one of us in order to show and tell us who He is and who we are (John 1:14). There could be no higher or more majestic picture of persuasion than God's condescension in Jesus Christ, the Son of God and the Son of man.

JESUS, *PATHOS*, AND PERSUASION

It should help us recognize the central importance of persuasion if we see, not only the person of Christ as Himself the climactic persuasion of God, but also the teaching of Christ as the most masterful and perfect example of what apologetic persuasion is. A couple of examples of this in Scripture should help us see the genius of Jesus as the Perfect Defender and Persuader.[1]

Jesus among the Religious Leaders

We will take two examples from Luke's Gospel, chapter 20. In the week before Christ's passion and resurrection, the religious leaders were particularly intent on trapping Him, and on undermining His authority, so that their own authority would be restored among the people.

> One day as Jesus was teaching the people in the temple courts and proclaiming the good news, the chief priests and the teachers of the law, together with the elders, came up to him. "Tell us by what authority you are doing these things," they said. "Who gave you this authority?" He replied, "I will also ask you a question. Tell me: John's baptism—was it from heaven, or of human origin?" They discussed it among themselves and said, "If we say, 'From heaven,' he will ask, 'Why didn't you believe him?' But if we say, 'Of human origin,' all the people will stone us, because they are persuaded that John was a prophet." So they answered, "We don't know where it was from." Jesus said, "Neither will I tell you by what authority I am doing these things." (Luke 20:1–8)

There is much that could be gleaned from the brilliance of Jesus in this encounter. We will focus our attention on the persuasive aspects of this apologetic challenge.

---

1. I am indebted to our pastor, Larry Westerveld, for many of these insights. Readers interested in filling out these and other truths in the life of Jesus are encouraged to access his sermons at https://www.trinityopchurch.org/sermons-and-links/sermons.

Jesus is in the temple teaching and "proclaiming the good news." At this point in Jesus's ministry, it is impossible to deny that He has accomplished great and miraculous works among them. So, the religious leaders approach Him, and they are no doubt convinced that they can undermine all that He has done.

They know that Jesus is certain that He acts according to God's will. All they need Him to do is to repeat that in the temple, and as the religious leaders, they will have "good grounds" to repudiate His entire ministry as blasphemous, and to arrest Him. After all, they think that they are the only ones who hold, and who alone can attest to, God's authority.

We should note here, given our previous discussions, that the religious leaders are demonstrating what it means for the image of God to be distorted and perverted. They are attempting to "subdue" Jesus, by asserting their own religious authority. Their authority, as Jesus will make clear to them, is based only on itself. They have no legitimate authority from God, since they have distorted His Word to them. Their attempt to subdue Him is a picture of sin's dominion over them.

The battle lines are drawn. It is time for Jesus to defend Himself and to confront them with the truth, even as they confront the Truth Himself. The religious leaders want to trap Jesus, to persuade the people that their views are legitimate and that Jesus's own teaching is false. So what we see here is Jesus the Apologist and Jesus the Persuader.

Jesus would not be trapped by these leaders; they could not fool Him by their questions. Instead, Jesus brilliantly trapped the would-be trappers with His own question.

We need to pause here to notice the persuasive character of Jesus's response. If we hurry past these details too quickly, we might not catch it. The religious leaders are seeking to undermine Jesus's authority by asking Him to identify where that authority comes from. Jesus could have answered them by telling them that He has authority from His Father (see Luke 10:22). That would have been perfectly correct and appropriate.

But Jesus knew something of the *pathos* of the crowd that surrounded

Him. He knew that many of them had believed the testimony, and thus the *authority*, of what John the Baptist had proclaimed in the wilderness. Jesus also knew that if the religious leaders had accepted the testimony of John, they would also accept His own testimony. So, the way to "connect" with these religious leaders in order persuasively to answer them is to pursue the question of authority.

Jesus addresses their question of authority with another question about authority. This is a crucial aspect of persuasion that we should not miss. *They* are the ones who approached Jesus with the issue of authority. Jesus could have bypassed their issue and approached them in any number of ways. Instead, he takes *their very issue* and challenges them according to it. In that way, Jesus is actually addressing the issue *they themselves* have chosen, but not in the way they had planned.

Jesus pursues their chosen topic of authority with a question. His question will both appeal to the *pathos* of the crowd listening, and it will persuasively trap the religious leaders within their own self-appointed authority. So, Jesus says He might agree to answer their question, but only if they could first answer His—Was the baptism of John from heaven or from man? Why this question?

The genius of the question can be seen when we recognize the people and place of this incident. Perhaps a more current analogy will help. Suppose, for example, that you are invited to preach by the youth group of a church. This is a church that has long ago denied the fundamental doctrines of Christianity. You come to that church and you preach the gospel with all the authority of Scripture itself. After preaching, the youth group rushes to the front of the church, with great appreciation and thanks for your message. They ask everyone in the church to join them in celebration of the truth of Scripture. They even ask you for an encore; they want to hear more.

But the elders of the church, sitting and seething together in the front pew, are incensed. They immediately move to the front of the church, grab the microphone from your hand, instruct the congregation to be seated, and then ask you this question: "By what authority do you dare to preach to this congregation? How dare you presume to tell them that Jesus Christ is the only way to heaven!" How might you respond to this question?

One way to respond would be to say, "I preach by the authority of God himself, who has spoken in every word of Scripture." That would be a true response, and there is nothing in that response that would be improper.

But another, perhaps more persuasive, response would be something like this: "I would be happy to discuss by what authority I have spoken in your church, but before I do, I would like to hear you respond to this question: By what authority do you deny that Jesus Christ is the only way to God?"

Can you see the point? If the elders respond that they deny that Christ is the only way because of what Scripture says, then they point to the authority of Scripture itself, which, as it happens, serves to approve your own preaching. Then a debate could ensue on the meaning of John 14:6, for example. If they respond by saying that the church's authority is a matter of their own studied conclusions, then they confess to being their own, final authority, and thereby deny the authority of God's very Word. This would make explicit what some in the church might not have realized.

Jesus's response shows the subversive beauty of the art of persuasion. As we have said, one of the key elements of persuasion is making a connection between the differing parties involved. Jesus makes this connection through speech, a connection through His own character, His *ethos*. What connection does Jesus make by asking His question?

Jesus knew that these teachers rejected His authority. We should remember as well that to reject Jesus's authority is to reject the ministry of John the Baptist (see Luke 3:15–19; 7:24–33; 9:19; 16:16). And to reject the ministry of John the Baptist is to reject the message of the Old Testament. Jesus knew that many in His audience would have recognized this. He knew their *pathos*.

John the Baptist had proclaimed that Jesus was the Messiah. John baptized Jesus in order to inaugurate His messianic ministry. John also told the crowds that he was not the Messiah, but that Jesus was, and that Jesus would baptize not with water, but with the Holy Spirit. John made it clear that his ministry was to "link" the Old Testament with the coming Messiah. If John's ministry was a false and misleading ministry, then Jesus was not the Messiah, and His own ministry was a farce.

Jesus knew that many in the surrounding crowd who were listening to this exchange were people who had believed John's message. They had concluded that John the Baptist was a prophet. If that is true, then it is a very short step to recognize that John inaugurated the messianic ministry of Jesus. That messianic ministry was the fulfillment of everything the Old Testament said (see Luke 24:44).

So, Jesus knows the *pathos* both of the surrounding crowd, as well as of his questioners. He knew His audience well. The crowd recognizes John the Baptist as a prophet. In that recognition, they likely have a genuine interest in, perhaps even a commitment to, Jesus's own ministry, as that ministry was announced by John. The questioners, on the other hand, presume to have the ultimate authority; they have no time for John the Baptist, for the crowd's curiosity, or for Jesus's ministry. Their hope would be to persuade the listeners as they confront and trap Jesus in His own teachings.

The questioners want to "persuade" Jesus; they want to trap Him. We could call this the "Persuasive Pinch." It is a "pinch" because it seeks to show that *one's own beliefs* "pinch" him between a rock and a hard place. It pushes a person to see the uncomfortable, perhaps even unlivable, constraints of his own beliefs. It is a *persuasive* pinch because the "natural" response would be to try to escape the self-induced trap and to move to another place, to extricate yourself from the rock and the hard place. Like a caged animal, the persuasive pinch should motivate you to free yourself from the trap and move to another position.

In this case, the questioners thought they could trap Jesus into a bold and explicit claim that He has the very authority of God Himself. If He said such a thing, they thought they would have grounds to arrest Him, because to them, no mere man could possibly be God, and so claiming

139

to be so was an offense to God and their own authority. If Jesus had said such a thing, of course it would have been true, but Jesus knew that this was not the time or place for such a claim. He could not be trapped into such a confession at this point. The questioners sorely underestimated the divine wisdom of the Savior.

Instead, Jesus turns the tables on them. He places His questioners into their own "persuasive pinch." He forces them to face the implications of their own beliefs, especially as those beliefs clash with what God has said in the Old Testament, as well as with the sympathies, the *pathos*, of the surrounding audience. He has brilliantly "pinched" them between their own presumed authority and the *pathos* of the listening crowd.

> They discussed it among themselves and said, "If we say, 'From heaven,' he will ask, 'Why didn't you believe him?' But if we say, 'Of human origin,' all the people will stone us, because they are persuaded that John was a prophet." So they answered, "We don't know where it was from." Jesus said, "Neither will I tell you by what authority I am doing these things." (Luke 20:5–8)

Notice again how Jesus's question shows us that Jesus recognized the disposition of His audience; He recognized their *pathos*. He knew the crowd affirmed John as a prophet. He also knew that the questioners not only denied John's prophetic ministry, but they denied the messianic ministry that John announced and that Jesus was carrying out. In that sense, they denied the very thing that they claimed as their own expertise, the Scriptures.

In denying these things, Jesus knew that these "chief priests" and "teachers of the law" were actually basing their entire religious program on their own, assumed, authority, rather than on the authority of God and His Word. Jesus knew all of this, and that knowledge was the foundation of his persuasion, and His question to them.

The very fact that they could not answer His question exposed them for the hypocrites they were. It showed the crowd that the leaders had no authority beyond their own personal pretense. They were not, as they claimed to be, representatives of God. Their authority went no further than their own selfish presumptions.

Because of Jesus's question, they were, indeed, in a "pinch." They had no place to go, no answer to give. This "pinch" should have moved them out of the corner in which they had trapped themselves, and to Jesus Himself. Instead, they wanted to arrest him (Luke 20:19). But Jesus's effort to pinch them according to the *pathos* of their own hypocrisy and the *pathos* of the audience was successful. They were left speechless; they could not defend their own presumed authority. In this way, there was a tacit admission of the authority of Jesus, which John himself had preached.

This incident reminds us that the *fact* of actual persuasion is always and everywhere the prerogative of the Lord Himself. Even if those to whom we speak are not actually persuaded of the truth of Christianity, that does not mean we have not been persuasive. We may have succeeded in showing someone that there is no place to turn but to Christ. We may have "pinched" them between a rock and a hard place, based on their own beliefs. That "pinch" should motivate them to free themselves, and to accept the truth that we offer. They can only do that, as we have seen, if the Holy Spirit uses the truth we communicate to change their hearts. But even if He does not change them, they remain in a pinch, and thus may be motivated, by the Spirit, to free themselves another time.

Even as He was the Master Defender and Persuader, some still would not believe. This in no way indicates a failure on the part of Jesus. His response was perfect and it accomplished all that was needed at that time. Even if the "authorities" would not turn to Christ, they could no longer assert their authority with impunity. Jesus had undermined the very foundations of their man-made religion. They had nothing to say to Him in response. The persuasion of the Savior had rendered them silent.

Jesus and the Sadducees

One more example of the Perfect Defender and Persuader will be useful for us to see. In this same chapter, we read:

The Faithful Apologist

Some of the Sadducees, who say there is no resurrection, came to Jesus with a question. "Teacher," they said, "Moses wrote for us that if a man's brother dies and leaves a wife but no children, the man must marry the widow and raise up offspring for his brother. Now there were seven brothers. The first one married a woman and died childless. The second and then the third married her, and in the same way the seven died, leaving no children. Finally, the woman died too. Now then, at the resurrection whose wife will she be, since the seven were married to her?" Jesus replied, "The people of this age marry and are given in marriage. But those who are considered worthy of taking part in the age to come and in the resurrection from the dead will neither marry nor be given in marriage, and they can no longer die; for they are like the angels. They are God's children, since they are children of the resurrection. But in the account of the burning bush, even Moses showed that the dead rise, for he calls the Lord 'the God of Abraham, and the God of Isaac, and the God of Jacob.' He is not the God of the dead, but of the living, for to him all are alive." Some of the teachers of the law responded, "Well said, teacher!" And no one dared to ask him any more questions. (Luke 20:27–40)

Jesus knew, as Luke tells us, that His questioners did not believe in the resurrection. They approach Jesus with what they think is a "trap" for anyone who *does* believe in a resurrection. They think that they will persuade Jesus of their view by trapping Him with His own view of the resurrection. They attempt their own persuasive pinch, based on what they know about Jesus's view of the resurrection of the dead.

Here is a group of religious leaders, prominent in the community, who not only deny the resurrection, but they also deny the existence of angels and demons. And they have no time for the prophets and psalms of the Old Testament. They claim to stake their reputation and their religion on the first five books of Moses alone.

Contrary to what we might be tempted to think, the first concern of the Sadducees, in their question, was not about marriage. They used a

142

marriage illustration to try to show how ludicrous a belief in the resurrection was. Their illustration had its focus in one of their "favored" books, Deuteronomy.

In Deuteronomy 25:5–6 it says:

> If brothers dwell together, and one of them dies and has no son, the wife of the dead man shall not be married outside the family to a stranger. Her husband's brother shall go in to her and take her as his wife and perform the duty of a husband's brother to her. And the first son whom she bears shall succeed to the name of his dead brother, that his name may not be blotted out of Israel. (ESV)

Because the Sadducees denied a resurrection from the dead, they needed to construe a way for life to continue by other means. Based on this passage, the Sadducees taught that the way to "live forever" was by way of *family progeny*. This is a crucial point to recognize as they approach Jesus. This is another place where Jesus is keenly aware of the *pathos* of His questioners.

If we properly see the *pathos* of these questioners, we will recognize that the problem they present to Jesus was not, centrally, a problem of *marriage* in the afterlife, but the more specific problem (given their skewed view of Scripture) of how *progeny* could continue if there *is* a resurrection.

Here was a woman, in their example, who, despite having the fullest opportunity to conceive, had never had children. The first man's name was "blotted out of Israel" because of this woman's infertility. How, the Sadducees are asking Jesus, will a "resurrection" rectify this situation?

If there is a resurrection, how will these seven work out which will be assigned to carry on the family? In other words, out of the fullness of opportunities—seven husbands—which one will be assigned, in the resurrection, to carry on the name with a woman who is wholly infertile? How can there be children in the resurrection, they are asking, when this woman has no chance of child-bearing?

Or, we could rephrase their question this way, in light of Deuteronomy

25 above: "Deuteronomy requires marriage within the family if one's name is to continue, and not be blotted out, in Israel. This woman, therefore, *must* be the wife of one of the brothers. But none of the brothers could continue the man's name by producing a son. And if none of them can produce progeny, *won't she have to marry 'outside the family' in the resurrection and thus break the law in Deuteronomy?*" Their question is meant to show the absurdity of a belief in the resurrection of the dead. How can resurrection "solve" what was (to them) such an intractable problem? This is their attempt persuasively to "pinch" Jesus into a corner.

It is their last question that prompts Jesus's initial response to the Sadducees. Again, the actual question of the Sadducees is meant to mock the notion of a resurrection, and to show it to be contrary to the law (in their case, to the five books of Moses). So, the question again is something like, "Won't this woman need to marry outside the family in order to have a chance at having a son, and thus in the resurrection go against the law of God and against God's plan for the continuation of Israel?"

This is why the first point that Jesus makes is that "those who are considered worthy of taking part in that age and in the resurrection from the dead will neither marry nor be given in marriage." If we think the question is about marriage, we miss the punch of the response Jesus gives. Their question is about the continuation of Israel *within* the family of Israel, as the law requires, and it is meant to show that belief in a resurrection defies what God has said about Israel.

Because Jesus perfectly understands this about his questioners, He is a Perfect Persuader, and a Perfect Apologist. He aims to defend the truth of the resurrection, but persuasively, that is, with the Sadducees' *own concerns* in view.

Notice that Jesus first points them to the resurrection, not as a continuation of the earthly family of Israel, but to the resurrection as itself containing "God's children." Those in the resurrection are God's children "because they are children of the resurrection." In this response, Jesus assures them of an eternal progeny, but it is a progeny in which God is their Father. This, again, is the pinnacle of divine wisdom, as we would expect from Jesus. His questioners cannot rise above earthly families and earthly fathers, but earthly fathers are not the central concern in the resurrection.

In other words, Jesus is saying to the Sadducees, "Are you troubled by the continuation of Israel in the face of infertility? You should recognize that there is no need for child-bearing in the resurrection *because those in the resurrection themselves are children of God!* As with the angels, there is no need for procreation, because life itself will continue forever."

Far from the notion that the resurrection presents a *problem* for the continuation of Israel, Jesus tells them that the resurrection is itself *the very continuation of Israel*. There is no need for marriage in the resurrection, because those who are there are children of God, and they will never die. In the resurrection, there is *progeny forever*. This is apologetics in action, a brilliant defense of the Christian faith. And it is masterful persuasion from the Master of persuasion Himself.

Jesus's final point to the Sadducees puts them in a very difficult spot; it effectively reverses the "persuasive pinch" that His questioners sought to produce. Jesus quotes from another "legitimate" book of theirs, Exodus, which is furthermore a central book in all of the Old Testament. He does so in order to point out to them just exactly how their own reading was deficient, and how they were supposed to read it.

"Speaking of Moses," He, in effect, says to them, "would God have identified himself as the God of Abraham, Isaac, and Jacob if those men were dead?" Could your God be the God of those who are not even alive? Why would God identify Himself as a God to men who no longer even exist? How could God say such a thing unless these men continue to live? In this way, Jesus uses *their own* presumed religion against them. In recognizing the *pathos* of the Sadducees, He uses what they affirm to challenge their beliefs.

Furthermore, it would not have escaped the notice of the Sadducees that the three men Jesus mentions—Abraham, Isaac, and Jacob—each had wives who struggled with infertility. Not only was God able to overcome those challenges within each family, but overcoming those infertility issues was for the purposes of the resurrection and eternal life of Abraham, Isaac, Jacob, and all their descendants who would believe in Him, not simply toward family progeny on earth.

In this incident, Jesus could have pointed to the truth in Scriptures that the Sadducees did not believe, to the Prophets or to the Psalms. But He chooses instead, persuasively, to face their challenge by addressing them *within* their own belief context—their *pathos*.

Jesus's persuasive apologetic used the truth of Scripture, truth the Sadducees themselves claimed to believe, to "connect" with the challenge of the Sadducees. He used their own presumed expertise to show them the fatal error of their thinking. He used their own words and beliefs against them. They were caught in a persuasive pinch.

If Exodus is true, says Jesus, then Abraham, Isaac, and Jacob must still be living. And, given what Jesus has already said, if they are living, then they remain and will forever be "children of God." There is no need for "marriage or giving in marriage" in eternity; those who are there are there because they are children of God, and they will never die. As Matthew reports in his telling of this story, Jesus's answer actually demonstrated to them that they were wrong because, as a matter of fact, they did not know the Scriptures or the power of God (Matt 22:29).

This is marvelous and magnificent persuasion from our Savior. So much so that Luke tells us the religious leaders quit trying to trap Him because they marveled at His answer (Luke 20:26) and "they no longer dared to ask him any question" (20:40 ESV). Undoubtedly, they "felt the pinch." They were not interested in being trapped again. As in the previous incident, they had nothing left to say.

Jesus, the Great Persuader

In both of these encounters, Jesus was aware of the assumptions, ideas, and beliefs of His audience, their *pathos*. He used those assumptions in ways that made His questioners feel the "pinch." In the first encounter, Jesus took the notion of authority and turned it against His questioners. He did that by taking the topic of authority and asking a question that His questioners would not answer. He knew the crowd was in favor of John the Baptist and his ministry. And He knew that if His questioners admitted that John's ministry came with the authority of heaven, then so also did His. He knew the *pathos* both of His audience and of His questioners.

In the second encounter, His argument was more subtle and thus utterly subversive. First, He would not allow the Sadducees to interpret what the resurrection would be like. They thought it would have to include the continuation of progeny so that Israel itself would continue. But Jesus denied their assumption, in His insistence that there is no need for marriage in eternity. Progeny continues, He tells them, because those who are resurrected are "children of God." It is precisely *because* of the resurrection that Israel's progeny will continue. Those who are resurrected are God's children forever.

He continues His persuasive pinch by taking from their very own authoritative Scriptures, the book of Exodus, and showing how that book affirms that the fathers of Israel—Abraham, Isaac, and Jacob—continue to live, though they have died. Thus, Israel lives on as the "children of God" even after they die.

With the Sadducees, Jesus could have easily told them that He Himself *was* the resurrection. Their disbelief in the resurrection was equivalent to their disbelief in Him as He was revealed in the Old Testament. But instead of choosing that route, Jesus appealed to the very things that the Sadducees themselves claimed to believe in order to show the deficiencies of their own beliefs.

He recognized, in the first place, that their question had its foundation in Deuteronomy (which was one of the few books they held to be authoritative). So, He answered them according to that foundation, reminding them that those who were faithful in Israel were, and would always be, "children of God." He then referred them to Exodus (another book they accepted) in order to challenge the logic of their rejection of the resurrection. How could it be, He asks them, that God could be the God of Abraham, Isaac, and Jacob, if they are dead and gone? Could God be the God of someone who does not exist?

The Sadducees had created an artificial doctrinal system that they thought could guarantee "eternal" life. It was a system that they believed was consistent with the Pentateuch, their Scriptures. Jesus masterfully demonstrates to them that the very books that they affirm to be true have been grossly misunderstood by them. Eternal life has its roots in the God who gives life to His people. They should have seen this, even in the few books that they deemed to be true. The life that God gives, from the garden forward, could only continue if God, by His grace, guaranteed it. Because of sin, it could never continue through our own strength.

In both of the occasions that we have looked at, Jesus recognizes the *pathos* of His audience, and He uses what they themselves have accepted in order to turn the tables on them. He persuasively "pinches" them between what they claim and what they should have seen according to their own belief systems. The pinch was keenly felt, because on each occasion, Jesus's opponents were silenced. Their own questions were exposed for their foolishness.

When challenges come to us, few of us will be able, naturally and automatically, to employ the divine wisdom and subversion of our Savior. However, if we listen to those challenges and consider them in light of the assumptions and beliefs that are behind them, we can begin to take into account the *pathos* of those who challenge us. It may be that the *pathos* is the road to a persuasive defense of the truth.

PAUL, *PATHOS*, AND PERSUASION

One of the most obvious biblical examples of a persuasive Christian apologetic is given to us in Paul's encounter with the Athenians in Acts 17:16–32. Instead of quoting the entire section as a whole, we will introduce its context and then highlight the portions relevant to our focus on *pathos*.

Luke tells us that Paul is in Athens waiting for Silas and Timothy to join him. He is in Athens because he has had opposition to his ministry and so was taken to Athens to remove him from some of that opposition.

Because of this opposition, we might think that Paul would lay low and just wait. But, instead, Paul commenced his ministry in Athens by reasoning both in the synagogue and in the marketplace (17:17).

As he defends the gospel, we're told that he stirs up curiosity, and some opposition, by preaching about Jesus and the resurrection (17:18). Luke tells us the philosophers are there and are skeptical about Paul's message. Though they think his message to be nothing more than confusing "babble" (17:18), they nevertheless want to hear more of what Paul has to say. So, ". . . they took him and brought him to a meeting of the Areopagus, where they said to him, 'May we know what this new teaching is that you are presenting?'" (17:19).

Mars Hill was a centuries-old location northwest of Athens that overlooked "the marketplace." Though some English translations insert that Paul was taken to "a meeting" of the Areopagus (NIV, vv. 19, 22), the Greek text does not explicitly say that there was a meeting, but simply says that Paul was taken "to the Areopagus" (see, for example, the ESV). So, it is unclear whether or not the council that normally ruled at the Areopagus was there when Paul spoke. Whether they were there or not, it is clear that Paul's address on that hill was under scrutiny by the Athenians and philosophers who had heard him speak in Athens.

There are three key aspects of persuasion in Paul's address that will be useful for us to highlight, especially as each of them reflects on the *pathos* of persuasion. Notice how Paul begins (Acts 17:22–23 TNIV):

> Paul then stood up in the meeting of the Areopagus and said: "People of Athens! I see that in every way you are very religious. For as I walked around and looked carefully at your objects of worship, I even found an altar with this inscription: to an unknown god. Now what you worship as something unknown I am going to proclaim to you.

First, Paul begins his address by *connecting* with his audience. He publicly recognizes that they are a "religious" people. In using this word, Paul is acknowledging the importance of the culture of Athens. He is letting them know that he has not been holed up, privately waiting to move on from Athens. Instead, he has taken an interest in their city and has taken note of the plethora of idols present. As one aspect of their *pathos*, Paul knows that there is a strong "religious" element in their entire city.

The importance of this point for persuasion should not be underestimated. Paul could have simply stood up at Mars Hill and called on everyone in his audience to repent. He will do that, eventually, but instead of opening with that, he wants them to know that he has taken a particular interest in their city and its history.

When we are considering a persuasive apologetic, one of the first things we should attempt to do is to understand the culture of the one(s) to whom we speak. One way to do this is to ask questions that can give us an inroad into the context of our interlocutors. Normally, when we meet someone for the first time, we almost immediately ask, "What do you do?" This can be a helpful question for starting to learn about them and establishing a connection.

Another question that may not immediately come to mind would be to ask, for example, "Where did you grow up?" or "Tell me about your family while you were growing up." These kinds of questions can give us a window into the lives and backgrounds of people we speak to, and they can give us points of connection as we demonstrate an interest in their experiences and familiarize ourselves with their point of view.

As Paul familiarized himself with Athenian culture, he came across an idol that was labeled "To an Unknown God." This provided a perfect point of persuasion for Paul. He knew he was in a culture that prized philosophy and that was enamored with knowledge. This, no doubt, was one of the reasons that "all the Athenians and the foreigners who lived there would spend their time in nothing except telling or hearing something new" (Acts 17:21 ESV). Luke tells us they craved new knowledge so much that they would spend their time in "nothing except" telling or hearing new things. Knowledge was a central aspect of Athenian culture, and Paul recognized that.

As Paul recognizes this almost inexhaustible thirst for knowledge in his audience, he draws them into his address by telling them that they can hear something "new" about this "Unknown God." They can hear who this God actually is.

In other words, Paul tells them that what he is about to declare to them will give them the opportunity to *know* that which they have decided is unknown. This is a brilliant subversive twist employed by the apostle. How could a city such as Athens balk at the opportunity to hear something "new" with respect to this Unknown God? Paul understood his audience; he knew their *pathos*. And he takes that knowledge and uses it as a point of persuasion in the beginning of his address.

A second aspect of Paul's appeal to the *pathos* of his audience is given in what Paul does next. This might initially look like anything but persuasion. Here he is in the midst of an entire audience of idol worshipers, and Paul begins by highlighting for them some of the most difficult teachings concerning God's own character (17:24–27):

> The God who made the world and everything in it is the Lord of heaven and earth and does not live in temples built by human hands. And he is not served by human hands, as if he needed anything. Rather, he himself gives everyone life and breath and everything else. From one man he made all the nations, that they should inhabit the whole earth; and he marked out their appointed times in history and the boundaries of their lands. God did this so that they would seek him and perhaps reach out for him and find him, though he is not far from any one of us.

Why would Paul begin his address this way? By now, we should recognize what Paul is doing, and why this section could be persuasive to his audience.

We remember, in Romans 1:18–20, that Paul affirms that all people know God. There is, therefore, in the heart of every individual person the true knowledge of God. That knowledge, as we have seen, is surely suppressed, but it is never completely eradicated. In our sin, we attempt to hold it down and we hope never to acknowledge it.

But, no matter how deep the suppression, the knowledge of God and His requirements *remains* in us. That knowledge, as Paul describes it, is of God's "invisible qualities—his eternal power and divine nature" (Rom 1:20). When we recall this in light of what Paul is doing at Athens, we are able to see something of Paul's strategy. Since the knowledge of God that all people have by virtue of God's revelation in creation is of His "eternal power and divine nature," Paul wants to describe those aspects of God's character to the Athenians.

So, he begins with creation and providence (aspects of God's "eternal power"). Since Paul is speaking to those in a Greek philosophical context, his point, given the Athenian *pathos*, takes account of this. This is not an affirmation of the eternity of creation, as Aristotle would have proposed. Neither is it a philosophically convoluted notion of a Demiurge emanating from the One, as neo-Platonists might suppose. Instead, Paul states unequivocally that God is the One who made the world and everything in it. There is nothing that is outside the scope of God's sovereign, creative activity.

Since He created all things, God is the "Lord of heaven and earth." The inescapable truth of Paul's opening statements would have, no doubt, been sobering to his audience. If God created all things, and is the ruler over all that He created, there is no escaping the fact that those who are created by Him are also accountable to Him. If He is Lord of heaven and earth, that means that He is Lord of the Athenians as well. He rules, not simply over Paul, or over the Jews, but He rules over *all people*. He is Lord *of heaven and earth*.

We should remember that Paul is, in one sense, "reminding" his audience of things they already knew. This would not be new information to them. God Himself has made sure that they would know these things about Him. The persuasive aspect of Paul's address can be seen as he "reaches in" to the very heart of every person listening, in order to bring out, if the Lord wills, the knowledge that God has already placed there.

The Athenians and the Suppressed Knowledge of God

Another dimension of Paul's strategy includes his understanding of the idols that fill the culture of Athens. How would Paul have understood this culture of idolatry? Fortunately, we don't have to guess at an answer to this question. Luke tells us that Paul "was greatly distressed to see that the city was full of idols" (Acts 17:16).

Paul tells us in Romans 1 what the suppression of the knowledge of God actually looks like in individual lives and in society. Suppression includes the fact that, in our sins, we "exchanged the glory of the immortal God for images made to look like a mortal human being and birds and animals and reptiles" (Rom 1:23). As Paul sees the idolatry of Athens, he knows that the making of idols is not done out of *ignorance* of God. Instead, it is rock-solid evidence that there is a suppression of the *knowledge* of God. That suppression cannot be content with no gods; it presents itself as worship, but it is worship of gods that are rooted and grounded in us and in our rebellion against God and His revelation.

This truth should help us watch out for various avenues of persuasion that might be available to us. There is a curious mood that often takes hold in our society. On the one hand, it is sometimes said that people are, generally speaking, *apathetic* about life. They really don't care to discuss truth, or goodness, or meaning, or goals for their lives. On the other hand, everyone seems to have an opinion about everything these days— and usually a strong one. Much of social media has become a platform for strong and caustic opinions, vitriol, personal attacks, and definitive positions.

These two poles are instructive for us. A suppression of the truth might *hope for* the possibility of apathy. If we could just convince ourselves that we don't care about much of anything, then we can avoid any "big" questions. We can just carry on with our day-to-day lives, all the while pushing down, as far as possible, the knowledge of God that bombards us like a flood with every breath we take.

But, when we take out our computers or phones and think about how we might best express ourselves, we suddenly care very deeply about things that are going on in the world, in our country, in our neighborhoods, and in our lives. Once we recognize this depth of concern from others, we ought to interpret it as a sign of (at least possible) idolatry. It may be that the reason there is such deep and definitive concern is because the issues that we seek to definitively address have become something of an idol to us.

Paul is clear in Romans 1 that it is not possible for a person made in God's image *not* to worship (Rom 1:25). A suppression of the knowledge of God cannot mean that worship itself is forsaken. No, as image-bearers of God, we are worshipers. That is, in part, what defines the image. But, if we refuse to acknowledge what we know, we will instead create another god, and so attach ourselves to that god, or gods, so that we tend to define our very lives by it. As with Paul, this idolatry should "greatly distress" us and prepare us to defend the Christian faith when the opportunity presents itself to us.

As Paul continues to "remind" his audience about who this God is, he makes two statements that would have seemed radical to this group of idol worshipers:

> And he is not served by human hands, as if he needed anything. Rather, he himself gives everyone life and breath and everything else. (Acts 17:25)

Here Paul has moved from the category of "eternal power" to God's "invisible attributes." This first statement highlights God's *aseity*. The aseity of God means that He, and He alone, is altogether *independent* and *self-sufficient*. Unlike the polytheism of Greek culture, there is no *quid pro quo* with the true God of Scripture. We do not give God something so that He might reciprocate and give us something as well. We do not bargain with God, or enter into negotiations with Him, as if we were His equal.

Instead, the true God needs nothing. Since He created all things, since He alone is Lord of heaven and earth, there can be nothing that He would need. He doesn't need us, or anything else, in order to be who

He is. He alone is the "I Am Who I Am" (Exod 3:14; see also John 8:58). As a matter of fact, says Paul, He is the One who alone gives to all people life and breath and everything else (Acts 17:25).

The implications of this truth would not have escaped Paul's audience. The true God needs nothing. Not only is He in need of nothing, but He gives everything that is needed for life to everyone. So the Athenians would have recognized Paul's point. Their very hearts beat at that moment, and they are able to take a breath, only because of God's own sovereign power and providence in their lives.

These were no "abstract" doctrines for the apostle. These truths about God have serious implications for the actual moment they hear them, as well as every other moment of their lives. Paul is telling them that, while the true God is utterly *independent*, they themselves are utterly and completely *dependent* on Him. They would have known this, because God makes Himself known in this way. And, they would have known that the idols surrounding Athens had no such qualities. Paul is showing their polytheism to be vain and useless.

We should pause for a moment to recognize how important the notion of "God" can be in our apologetic persuasion. An example from my own experience might be instructive here. One of my friends who is an unbeliever returned from overseas travel. The minute he saw me after his return, he said to me, with some fervor, "Your God does not exist. He *could not* exist, given the suffering that I saw when I was overseas!" I looked at him and asked him, "Do you think I believe in a God who is *responsible* for all of that suffering?" He just smiled at me and the conversation stopped—for the moment. A little while after that, as we were both scheduled to attend the same event, he said he wanted to pick me up and go with me to it. As soon as we got in his car, he wanted to know what I believed and why. It was a wonderful opportunity to present the gospel to him. I am personally confident that my question, which appealed to the *pathos* of his conception of God, sparked our further conversation.

The reason I asked him the question I did was because his own accusation against me presupposed that he and I had the same view of God.

This was a part of his *pathos*. He thought he knew enough about the God that I trust to accuse Him of the suffering he saw. Without going into all of the difficulties of the problem of sin and suffering in this world, I could confidently question him on the notion that God was not *responsible* for the effects of sin and evil in this world. Scripture is clear that we are the responsible agents of sin (e.g., Gen 2:16–17). That truth was a wonderful entrée to a discussion of the gospel.

I remember a man who was involved in an evangelistic ministry for intellectuals saying one time that whenever someone comes to him and says, "I don't believe in God," his first question is, "Tell me what kind of God you don't believe in. It may very well be that I don't believe in that God either!" This, too, is an example of taking *pathos* into account. Instead of responding immediately by saying why we believe in the Christian God, it is extremely helpful to know what kind of God it is that someone cannot accept. Again, this question brings to the fore what someone thinks about God; it taps into the *pathos* of one's understanding of God.

Even as Paul gets to the root of their presumed autonomy and idolatry, he also reminds them that they are who they are, as Athenians, because of the meticulous sovereignty of God:

> From one man he made all the nations, that they should inhabit the whole earth; and he marked out their appointed times in history and the boundaries of their lands. (Acts 17:26)

The apostle here affirms the common roots of all people. God made from Adam every nation so that we would inhabit the world that God made. In that sense, we are all connected by God's providential design.

But there are distinctions. And here Paul declares that all people live where they live because God has determined they would. In this, Paul destroys any pride the Athenians might have because they are in Athens. They are not Athenians because of any intrinsic superiority. They are Athenians due to the sheer determination and providence of a sovereign God.

This truth, of course, follows from the fact that God created all things and that He is the Lord of heaven and earth. He is not a God who is aloof from His creation. He has not set the world in motion and let it run on its own. That which He created, He governs.

All of this, thus far, is an appeal to the knowledge of God that is part and parcel of who these people are as those made in God's image. As Paul counters the rampant idolatry in Athens, he provides real (and intrinsically known) content to what they supposed was an "unknown god." Thus, there is real persuasion here, as the content Paul provides is content that God Himself provides while He makes Himself known to them through everything He has made. The *pathos* to which Paul appeals is the true knowledge of God and His requirements that all Athenians have.

The biblical lesson for us should be clear. It is never "out of place" for us to discuss God and His character with those who do not know Christ. We must discuss such things with "gentleness and reverence." And we must be careful to enter these discussions with biblical wisdom. There may be times when it is best not to discuss things like this in this particular way. But, when God and His character are discussed, they appeal to the *pathos* of our listeners. God has ensured this.

Even so, there should always be a focus on the fact that anyone to whom we speak is, by nature, one who knows God, but suppresses that knowledge. We can see this, for example, when national or personal tragedies occur, and those involved will often appeal to prayer. That appeal from those outside of Christ shows forth the true knowledge of God that all people have. So there will be an aspect of persuasion to any discussion about the true God and His character.

The third *pathos* aspect of Paul's address on Mars Hill is like the second, though a bit more specific. Paul decides to use something with which his audience is familiar:

"For in him we live and move and have our being." As some of your own poets have said, "We are his offspring." (Acts 17:28)

157

Paul here quotes the Greek writers Epimenides in the first quotation, and Aratus in the second. He did this, no doubt, recognizing the *pathos* of his audience. Surely most of them would have known these poets and their writings.

It might be instructive to note how Thomas Aquinas understands why Paul uses these quotes:

> Hence sacred doctrine makes use also of the authority of philosophers in those questions *in which they were able to know the truth by natural reason*, as Paul quotes a saying of Aratus . . . [2]

The question for us is whether or not Paul uses these quotations because he wants to affirm that these poets "were able to know the truth by natural reason." The question could be posed this way: "When Epimenides and Aratus wrote these statements, were they true?"

To answer that question, we would need to know to whom "him" refers in the first quote, and to whom "his" refers in the second. As it turns out, both men were referring to Zeus, and not to the true God. So, while their "natural reason" sought to affirm a god, the god affirmed was just another example of idolatry. The statements themselves could not be true in the way those poets wrote them. "Natural reason" was nothing more than sinful reason; it was able to produce only idolatry.

So why does Paul quote these two poets? This is Paul the master persuader. Not only does he know the general *pathos* of his audience, as he walked around Athens and was moved by their idolatry, but he knows their literature as well. And he knows that the reason that Epimenides and Aratus would have posited a god is the same reason that there were idols littering the landscape of Athens. It was because they know God but suppress that knowledge by creating other gods to worship.

But, in quoting these poets, doesn't the apostle affirm what these poets wrote? The answer is both yes and no. He affirms that they wanted

---

2. Thomas Aquinas, *Summa Theologica*, trans. by Fathers of the English Dominican Province, (Bellingham, WA: Logos Research Systems, Inc., 2009), I q.1 a.1 ad 2 (emphasis mine).

to acknowledge something that transcended the creation, something that was meant to provide significance and meaning to their otherwise mundane existence. Their affirmations were false, literally speaking, but their "aspirations" were correct; they knew the true God but suppressed that knowledge.

Paul also does not affirm what they wrote because Paul has just spent the initial part of his address *defining* who the true God is! As we have seen, his initial declaration affirmed the aseity, the sovereignty, and the all-encompassing providence of God. So, when Paul quotes their poets later in his speech, his audience at Athens would immediately recognize that Paul has changed the person to whom the two quotations referred (i.e., "him" and "his").

Instead of referring to Zeus, as the poets had done, they would have known that Paul was using these quotes to refer to the One he had just described, the Lord of heaven and earth. In other words, Paul takes a false product of "natural reason," which ends in idolatry, and transforms it to refer to the glorious truth of God Himself. "In Zeus we live and move and have our being" has been changed by Paul to, "In this true and sovereign and *a se* God we live and move and have our being." Similarly, "we are Zeus's offspring" now changes to "we are the offspring of the Creator of all that is."

Like his Savior, Paul is an apologist of persuasion. He not only communicates God's very truth to them, but he does so in a way that would have "connected" and resonated with their own individual *pathos*, as well as the *pathos* of their Greek culture.

Paul Completes His Apologetic

As Paul concludes his apologetic to the Athenians, there are a few more important points that Luke makes that deserve our brief attention. It is never enough in our apologetic simply to articulate who God is, even though such truths are crucial to understand. Since apologetics is a defense of the *Christian* faith, we should always have in view the truth of who Christ is and what He has done for us. That is, the Christian faith, in its proper affirmation of who God is, recognizes that our knowledge of God as He is given to us in the gospel requires a knowledge of who Christ is and what He has done. Notice, in this regard, how Paul finishes his address:

> Therefore since we are God's offspring, we should not think that the divine being is like gold or silver or stone—an image made by human design and skill. In the past God overlooked such ignorance, but now he commands all people everywhere to repent. For he has set a day when he will judge the world with justice by the man he has appointed. He has given proof of this to everyone by raising him from the dead. (Acts 17:29–31)

Paul completes his address by challenging the logic of idolatry itself. He challenges them with the inconsistency of their own principles. In effect, he says, "If you yourselves affirm that we are the offspring of the gods, how can it be that you attribute divinity to those things that *you* have made? How can you worship those things that *you* have made, when you believe that *you* are God's offspring?" Either you are God's offspring, or the gods you worship are your creations. Which is it? It can't be both.

Paul then sets his appeal for them to repent within the context of God's new covenant plan of redemption.[3] What he is saying to the Athenians is that the Lord of heaven and earth *now*, since Christ has come and completed His work, is commanding all people in every place to repent of their idolatry and disobedience.

This should not have surprised the Athenians. Surely, the one who created all people, who rules over all of His creation, who sets the places and boundaries of their habitation, in whom we all live and move and

---

3. What does Paul mean when he says that in the past, God overlooked ignorance? This may sound as though God was not concerned with unbelief in the past. However, we can compare what Paul says here with his similar address in Acts 14. There, in v. 16, he says, "In the past, he let all nations go their own way" (see also Rom 3:25). Paul is here describing in one sentence God's plan of salvation for His people. In the past, God set His sights on the nation of Israel. That was His sovereign design.

have our being, would require that we turn from our idolatry to worship Him alone. The Athenians would have already been familiar with their own guilt in this regard. Included in their knowledge of God, we remember, is knowledge of what He would require of us (Rom 1:32).

But then, Paul does something that both completes his apologetic, and also no doubt stirred up again the ire of some of his audience. We recall that it was Paul's preaching about Jesus and His resurrection in the marketplace that caused some of his listeners to ridicule him (Acts 17:18). We might think that Paul would avoid this topic, since it had caused such a negative reaction. But we know Paul better than that.

Rather than avoiding that negative topic, Paul goes back and explicitly addresses it. The resurrection, as a matter of fact, provides proof of everything Paul has been saying. It is the fact that there is One who alone has conquered death that should move the Athenians to believe what Paul is saying. Surely, the one who made all things and who rules over heaven and earth is capable of overcoming that most inevitable of human conditions.

If you really want to live, the apostle is saying, then it is time to repent and to turn to the author of life Himself. Not only is He alive, but He will come again, at the end of history, to judge whether or not we have repented and trusted Him. Jesus lives; He has come back from the dead. Trust Him, because you will face Him in judgment. Christian apologetics has its natural conclusion in Christ, His resurrection, and His return. Without that message, it is useless, and Paul knew that (see 1 Cor 15:12–19).

Finally, it is helpful that Luke lets us in on the responses of Paul's audience (Acts 17:32–34):

When they heard about the resurrection of the dead, some of them sneered, but others said, "We want to hear you again on this subject." At that, Paul left the Council. Some of the people became followers of Paul and believed. Among them was Dionysius, a member of the Areopagus, also a woman named Damaris, and a number of others.

As was the case in the marketplace, mention of the resurrection caused some of Paul's audience to sneer at him. This highlights the point we made in chapter 3 about God ultimately doing the persuading. No matter how persuasive *we* might be able to be in our defense of Christianity, it is the Spirit of God, working by and with the truth of His Word, who can change human hearts. People did not sneer at Paul because he was deficient in his communication on Mars Hill. They sneered because they would not receive the truth of God; they would not repent.

There were others, however, who wanted to hear more. This is a most encouraging sign, and we can trust that Paul made sure that they did hear more. The seed of God's truth was planted in them. Whether Paul's message fell on rocky soil or was deeply planted could not be seen at that point in history. But they did want to hear more, which means that God the Holy Spirit was continuing to work by and with Paul's message according to God's own sovereign purposes.

In addition to those who wanted to hear more, Luke also tells us that there were those who believed. Among them was a man, Dionysus, who sat on the council of Mars Hill and was responsible for judging the merits of addresses given there. We are not told if Dionysius was there that day as a judge, but we are told that he was a "member of the Areopagus," and the Lord converted him through Paul's message.

What Luke gives us here is the range of responses that we will experience in our own attempts persuasively to defend Christianity. There will be those who continue to sneer, others will want to hear more, and some, by God's grace, will be converted. But no matter the response, we should be clear that the goal of our persuasive defense is to communicate the truth of God, with gentleness and reverence, and with as much wisdom as the Lord might give us. With a Christian *ethos*, appealing to the *pathos* of our listeners, we want them to hear about Christ. If we have done that, then we can be confident that the Holy Spirit will use that truth according to His own sovereign will. And at no point will our communication of the Lord's truth be in vain. It will always accomplish God's good and sovereign purposes in those who hear it (Isa 55:10–11).

Paul's Persuasive Approach

Before we move on, let's summarize Paul's persuasive approach to a defense of Christianity as he addressed the Athenians. First, Paul recognizes the general culture of Athens. He walked around the city and was moved by their idolatry. In addressing that idolatry, he also affirmed that they were a "religious" people.

People are unavoidably religious by nature. This is part and parcel of what it means to know God. But the religion they adopt will always be idolatry until and unless they truly repent and put their faith in the true God. When we can, it is useful for us to detect the "culture" of those to whom we speak. What things do they cling to? What matters to them? What do they see as non-negotiable in their lives and in their thinking? Looking for answers to these questions can give us clues to their own idolatry.

Second, Paul moves directly to the character of God. Specifically, he highlights God's "eternal power and divine nature." He tells them God is their Creator; He is the One who is in need of nothing. He gives to them life, breath, and all things. He has determined their boundaries. He has brought humanity forth from one man. In Him alone all of us live and move and have our being.

These are "heady" aspects of God's character. If they simply came to the Athenians "out of the blue," these realities would be shocking to innocent ears. But they did not come "out of the blue" and they did not meet innocent ears.

They are things about God that God Himself had been revealing to them all along. They came to ears that would not acknowledge the truth that they were receiving through the things that were made. Even if the Athenians continued to reject Paul's message, which some of them did, these truths about God "connected" with the truth that God Himself implants in all of us. Paul knew the truth he was proclaiming would make its home in each of their hearts, even if they continued to reject it. The truth Paul proclaimed found its home in the Athenians' hearts, since in those hearts dwelt the knowledge of the true God.

Third, Paul knew some specific aspects of their literature and was able to use it to connect them to the truth of his message. This may not always be possible for us. We may meet someone whose particular interests and knowledge we won't know. But, like Paul, it would be useful to keep in mind how we might be able to connect to things that are more generally known—popular literature, movies, perhaps some of the latest news stories. Even if each of these aspects of Paul's persuasive message are not readily available to us, recognition of these principles should help us in our thinking about persuasion and its importance for our apologetic discussions.

Persuasion should attempt to discern the *pathos* of the audience when defending and commending the faith. There are a host of ways that this can be done, since there are a host of audiences. Perhaps a contemporary example might help illustrate the use of persuasive *pathos* to commend the faith.

A few years ago, my wife and I attended the Christmas worship service of a large, metropolitan church. Since it was Christmas, the place was packed to overflowing with people. As the service began, the very first thing that we did was stand and sing, "O Come All Ye Faithful." After the hymn, the minister walked to the pulpit and said something like this:

> That is a beautiful hymn, and it was enthusiastically sung by you all. But I want to make sure all of you are aware of what you just sang. Numerous times through that hymn, you all sang, "O come let us adore Him." I want you to know that we are here this morning for that very purpose. We are here to adore Jesus Christ who came and paid the penalty for sinners. He rose from the dead and now lives. He will return again to judge the living and the dead.
>
> Since you have all now sung those words, I want to ask you, Are you here to adore *that* Christ? I hope you are. But, if you are here only because it's Christmastime and you think you should go to church during this time, there are numerous churches around here where you

can go. This isn't one of those churches. We're here to worship the Savior whose coming Christmas celebrates. If you are here to adore the Savior, please continue to worship with us. If not, you might want to find one of those other churches.

Can you see the concern for *pathos* in this minister's statement? He was concerned to preach the good news of the gospel to this congregation during Christmas. But he was also aware of his audience. He knew there were very likely some who were there only because it was Christmastime. His statement was calculated to change their reason for being there, based on what they themselves had just sung. It took those words that they had sung in the hymn seriously. It urged them to commit themselves to the worship of Christ.

I looked around that morning and didn't notice anyone leaving. That doesn't mean everyone there decided to commit themselves to worship Christ. But it was made abundantly clear that everything in the worship service was designed for that very purpose.

This is a wonderful and strategic example of the importance of *pathos*. The entire audience had just sung about adoring Christ, the newborn King. The minister took those very words that the congregation sang and pushed them to a consistent application. He called the entire congregation to a commitment, based on what they themselves had just affirmed in that hymn. For those who were Christians that morning, it highlighted again why they were there. For those who were not Christians but who had sung that hymn, it challenged them to take the words they had sung deadly seriously. It took what might have been a "formality" for some—we go to church because it's Christmas—and turned it into an existential reality in that Christmas worship service.

The *pathos* of our audience is a crucial part of a persuasive apologetic that should not be overlooked. Without some knowledge of the *pathos* of our listeners, our words might simply float in the void.

SIX

LOGOS

In this last chapter, we return to where we began; we have come full circle. We began by highlighting the gracious condescension of the Lord at the beginning of time. There we saw that the Lord condescended to *speak*. Even as He *spoke* all of creation into existence, He determined to *speak* to Adam and Eve so that they would know how to love and serve Him in the garden He had made for them. That communication from the Lord to Adam and Eve connected Him to them, and them to Him, and helped provide for their covenant relationship.

LOGOS AND PROOFS

In this chapter, we come to the third and final aspect of persuasion. Our focus here will be on the *logos* of apologetic persuasion. When we focus on the *logos* of persuasion, as Aristotle's description says, we think about "proof, or attempted proof, provided by the *words* of the speech itself."[1] In other words, we are now at the point where we can think about what it means to *prove* what we want people to accept, and what the *content* of our proofs should be.

---

1. Aristotle, "Rhetorica," in *The Basic Works of Aristotle*, Richard McKeon, ed. (New York: Random House, 2009), 1601.

We might be tempted to think that once something is "proven," it is a solid and unalterable fact. Sometimes the notion of "proof" can lend itself to that idea. A proof, we might think, is something that is a certain fact that cannot be overturned.

But the notion of proof can be more complicated than that. There are a host of things associated with any proof that can sometimes be missed or ignored. For example, we recognize that water freezes at 32 degrees Fahrenheit. Though this can be "proven" by experiment, there are a number of situations that can arise to show this "fact" to be less certain than we might think. For example, the level of water's purity can alter its ability to freeze. One of the reasons deicing salt is added to streets on icy days is because salt added to water lowers the temperature at which it will freeze.

These situations don't necessarily alter our assertion that "water freezes at 32 degrees Fahrenheit," but they do help us recognize that such an assertion is one of probability—even if a high degree of probability—and not of certainty. A proof like this is not an "unalterable" fact, but instead is a "highly likely" fact.

The truth is, any proof that we offer that has its source in our experience, or in experience generally, is a *probable* proof; it has a particular likelihood to it. The reason for this is that experiences are, by definition, limited in a multitude of ways. The best such a proof can offer is a *probable* fact or truth.

This fact might wreak havoc on our typical understanding of proofs, especially since it is often assumed that it is illegitimate to assert anything at all unless it is susceptible to a strict proof. If we believe something but cannot find or offer a proof for it, some think that our belief is blind or without any real support. If we believe something and can only offer a probable proof for it, then we're told our belief must remain tentative. Even if the proof is *highly* probable, there still remains a possibility that it could be wrong.

This does *not* mean, we should emphasize, that proofs based on experience are, by definition, *unpersuasive*. As a matter of fact, experience-based proofs can be very persuasive, even though they might conclude something that is only probable. Just because water *may not* freeze at 32 degrees Fahrenheit does not mean that I should doubt that water will, in fact, freeze at that temperature at a given time and place.

The point, however, is that it is useful for us to recognize the limitations of the notion of proof, so that we better understand what we're doing when we seek to prove something. Proofs can be very useful, but we should not think that they are, in and of themselves, able to convince, especially when we're dealing with proofs of the Christian faith.

There are other important aspects to the notion of proof that we should be aware of. Let's take a standard proof, which is given in the form of a syllogism. A syllogism is a form of proof in which a conclusion is drawn from two premises:

Premise 1:   All men are mortal.
Premise 2:   Socrates is a man.
Conclusion: Socrates is mortal.

What would we say about this proof? We might initially think that it is utterly convincing, and that might be a proper way to view it. But, it is important to look at it a little more closely as we think about the actual persuasive force of proofs like this.

One of the first things we should recognize about a proof like this is the distinction between a *valid* proof and a *sound* proof. When we say a proof is *valid*, what we mean, technically speaking, is that *if* the premises are true, the conclusion will necessarily follow. Now, what do we want to say about this proof above? Is it valid? Yes, the conclusion seems to follow necessarily from the premises.

On the other hand, we deem a proof *sound* when it is a valid proof *and* it is determined that the premises *are*, in fact, true. So, a sound proof or argument is a *valid* argument whose premises are determined to be *true*. Is the above syllogism a *sound* proof? More than likely, we will answer yes to that question because we already thought it was valid, and each of the premises seem to be true on their own. If we say "yes, this is a sound proof," then we are saying that the proof is a *valid* argument in which the premises are, in fact, true.

Let's think about Premise 1. Our natural inclination is to affirm Premise 1 as obviously true. And with most people, there would be little reason to question its truth. But, remember what we said above about experience-based proofs. The best we can do with such proofs is conclude that it is *probably* true. Our experiences confirm that everyone dies, meaning they are mortal. However, our experiences, as well as the experiences of everyone else, are always limited.

So, when we say in Premise 1 that "All people are mortal," what we are actually affirming is that "Experience shows that all people die." When stated that way, we recognize the limitations of the statement. No one person, nor all people collectively, has been able to know and experience "all people." Premise 1 simply assumes that what has been seen to occur in all human experience, *always* occurs with all people. But, of course, there is no way to actually show the reality of Premise 1, since there is no *actual* record or experience of "all people."

As a matter of fact, for those of us who believe the truth of Scripture, we know that Enoch did not die (Gen 5:24; Heb 11:5). So, "All people are mortal" would have to be changed to "Almost all people are mortal." If by "All people are mortal" we mean that every person has died, that statement is false.

We noted above that a *sound* argument is a valid argument in which it is determined that the premises are true. Since we have a reason to deny Premise 1, must we now conclude that the syllogism is not sound? Not necessarily.

As long as we recognize that statements such as Premise 1 are *typically*, if not *universally*, true, we can also recognize the *persuasive* value of Premise 1. In other words, the purpose of the proof does not have to be objective *certainty*, so that there is no possibility of any variation whatsoever. Instead, the point of the proof is to bring someone to agree with the conclusion, even though every variable and permutation cannot be considered.

The point of this example is *not* to undermine these kinds of proofs. The point is for us to recognize that, while proofs can serve a legitimate purpose, we should not give them more weight than they can bear. We should not think that proofs are, in and of themselves, the only standard for a rational argument or a rational belief. They can play an important role, but much more is inevitably involved when discussions like this are taking place.

LOGOS AND APOLOGETIC PROOFS

When we are focusing on persuasive apologetics, we are interested not simply in generic proofs or syllogisms, but in how we might show others the *reasons* why we believe in Christianity. We want to be able to articulate a *rationale* for our trust in Christ. So, the proofs that we offer will have their focus in the truth that we believe about the Christian faith. Oftentimes, in the history of apologetics, this includes proofs for God's existence.

There is a centuries-long tradition of Christians offering various proofs for God's existence. In the early church, apologetics needed to focus on the rationale for Christianity, in the context of the intense persecutions that were being foisted on Christians.

Justin Martyr (ca. AD 100–165), for example, who is typically referred to as the church's first apologist, wrote an "Apology" to the emperor Antoninus Pius. His defense was a brilliant form of persuasion. He knew that the emperor was committed to ruling his empire *justly*. Justin chose this word—justice—as the "connection" he would make between him and the emperor. Justin appealed to that commitment of justice by the emperor so that the Christians who were being persecuted might begin to be treated *justly*. Justin challenges the emperor, for example, to observe the lives of the Christians and see if they are committing any crimes. If not, *justice* demands that persecution stop.[2]

---

2. For more on Justin and the history of apologetics, see William Edgar and K. Scott Oliphint, eds., *Christian Apologetics Past and Present: A Primary Source Reader (Volume 1: To 1500)* (Wheaton, IL: Crossway, 2009).

It was a brilliant persuasive defense. Justin knew two things—he knew that Antoninus Pius prided himself on a just rule of his empire. He knew that, at least on the surface, Pius was not approving persecution simply for its own sake. If persecution were taking place under Antoninus Pius, it would have to be a *just* persecution. Justin knew the *pathos* of Pius, and he chose a proper word—justice—in order to connect his argument to Pius.

Justin also knew that Christians were acting as good citizens; this was the Christian *ethos* of the day. They would not worship the emperor, of course, because they *could not* do that. But, neither were they committing crimes in the empire. They were seeking, as much as their commitment to Christ would allow, to be under the authority of the emperor. So, the *logos* of persuasion for Justin was *justice*. Pius was committed to it and Christians themselves were abiding by it. To persecute them simply because they were Christians was *unjust*. Justin knew it, and he wanted to "pinch" Pius between his own commitment to justice and the unjust treatment of Christians under his reign. He pinched him between a rock and a hard place, and that pinch introduced a motivation for Pius to change his behavior.

In the fourth century, and going forward, Christian persecution virtually ceased, and Christians had the opportunity to think and write about their faith in a more congenial environment. The great Augustine (354–430), for example, wrote his magnum opus, *The City of God*, in part, so that the church would not succumb to the pagan influences that had infiltrated it. This work is a masterful defense of the purity of Christianity, against idolatry, and of "the city of God" itself.

As time moved forward in the church, one of the arguments that gained some prominence in the Middle Ages, and that has become, for many, one of the "standard" ways to prove the existence of God, is the argument for God as the First Cause. The argument goes (something) like this:

1. Everything that comes to be has a cause.
2. The universe came to be.
3. Therefore, God caused the universe.

These three statements do not exhaust the argument, but are meant simply to set forth the main tenets of the argument from causality.

What should we think of this argument? Since our focus in this chapter is on the *logos* of persuasion, that is, on the persuasive force of the *words* that seek to prove God's existence, we should first ask about the force of the cause/effect relationship in this proof. In what way might these words be used to persuade? How could the notion of First Cause not simply present an argument, but *draw* someone into our discussion?

The first premise above should be obvious to anyone. By definition, anything that comes to be must come to be by virtue of something else that caused it. Nothing can cause itself and nothing can come to be by itself; there would need to be something else that *caused* it to exist.

The second premise can be controversial, for at least two reasons. The first reason was already mentioned above. Whenever there is a premise that relies on our own experience, it can only be probable. No one has ever experienced "the universe" in its entirety. The best we are able to do is to look at aspects of the universe and project what *might* have happened "in the beginning."

The second reason the second premise can be controversial is related to the first. Since no one can transcend "the universe" in order to see it as a whole, and since no one was "there" when the universe began, many scientists remain uncertain as to whether, or how, the universe had a beginning at all.

In the big bang theory, for example, it is thought that the universe went through an extended period of "inflation" as it expanded more and more. According to one scientist, however, "Inflation is an extremely powerful theory, and yet we still have no idea what caused inflation or whether it is even the correct theory."[3]

So, as scientists wrestle with the origin of the universe, the best that they are able to do is to look at its current state and then to project backward toward a *possible* explanation. But that is not satisfying to most

---

3. See Ker Than, "How Did the Universe Begin?," LiveScience, June 27, 2019, www.livescience.com/65819-how-did-the-universe-begin.html.

people who are interested in these kinds of questions. For them, the origin of the universe is a foundational question: "All other mysteries lie downstream of this question," said Ann Druyan, author and widow of astronomer Carl Sagan. "It matters to me because I am human and do not like not knowing."[4]

The persuasive advantage of the second premise, then, is that the origin of the universe is related to our own origins, and so it holds the promise of better explaining who we are, and why we're here in the first place. In other words, included in the notion of the origin of the universe is the origin of human beings. If we know how and why we began to exist, we can know something of who we actually *are*, and *why* we are here now. This gives us both identity and purpose.

The conclusion in proposition 3 above is that, therefore, God caused the universe. There are a number of things that should catch our attention about this conclusion. The first thing we recognize is that any Christian would give a hearty "Amen!" to this conclusion. For Christians, the two premises and the conclusion are as certain as our own existence.

This is one of the reasons, no doubt, that proofs like the causal proof have been so popular. As Christians, we rightly see that there is no rational option available than the one the First Cause argument provides for us. We recognize that the universe is unable to explain itself; it needs an explanation—a reason for its existence—that transcends its own existence.

It is important for us to recognize, however, that when we are attempting to defend the Christian faith, and to do it persuasively, we are not speaking to people who have a clear view of the way the world turns. As we have seen, we are speaking to people who have a vested interest in suppressing the obvious. Even though they see God both within and without, they continually hold down what they see, as they exchange the truth of God for a lie and so worship and serve created things. As a matter of fact, unless the Spirit of God changes them by the Word of God,

---

4. Than, "How Did the Universe Begin?"

they are willfully *unable* to see the world properly (see, e.g., John 3:3; Rom 8:1–5; 1 Cor 2:14).

Those who remain outside of Christ will "naturally," because of their sin, in and of themselves, want to mute the significance of this proof. One famous example of a proposed refutation of the First Cause argument came from the atheist British philosopher Bertrand Russell. It is worth reading him carefully at this point, as it shows us some possible weaknesses in the argument's persuasive capacity:

> I for a long time accepted the argument of the First Cause, until one day, at the age of eighteen, I read John Stuart Mill's *Autobiography,* and I there found this sentence: "My father taught me that the question, 'Who made me?' cannot be answered, since it immediately suggests the further question, 'Who made God?'" That very simple sentence showed me, as I still think, the fallacy in the argument of the First Cause. If everything must have a cause, then God must have a cause. If there can be anything without a cause, it may just as well be the world as God, so that there cannot be any validity in that argument.[5]

For a Christian, Russell's response is rightly seen to be irrational; it virtually gives up on a rationale for the universe. But we have to recognize that a certain "irrationality" is built into the unbelieving mind. Apart from Christ, as we exchange the truth of God for a lie, we are willing to substitute almost any idea for the one true answer, no matter how irrational it seems at the time.

Why would Russell agree with Mill that the First Cause proof would lead him to ask, "Who made God?" The reasoning goes something like this: whenever we speak to someone about the Christian faith, we should recognize that they have chosen to view the world around them, including themselves, without reference to God at all. So, from an unbelieving point of view, if we insert the notion of God into a proof, they will be

---

5. From Bertrand Russell, "Why I Am Not a Christian," The Bertrand Russell Society, https://users.drew.edu/~jlenz/whynot.html.

inclined to apply our own argument to that notion. If our argument has as its foundation the *ongoing continuity* of the cause/effect relationship, then it would be a "natural" question to ask about the cause of God's existence.

Or, to refer again to Russell's response above, if we're going to introduce a notion of "God" as uncaused to explain the universe, why not simply posit a universe that has no ultimate cause? In both cases, neither view is amenable to scientific testing. "The universe" as a whole cannot be subject to scientific testing because it is impossible to get outside of it, or to view it "as a whole." Why not just say, for all we know, that the universe has always been, and has always been causing a vast number of effects within it?

I remember discussing this argument with a Christian apologist years ago. I asked him why, *from the perspective of unbelief,* the notion of an uncaused universe could not be satisfactory. His only response was, "That doesn't explain the universe!" In other words, he was convinced that those outside of Christ would rather have an explanation for the universe as a whole than simply live with the fact that the universe as a whole remains a mystery with respect to its origins. But unbelief will always, of itself, default to an explanation *without God* rather than admit its own irrationality and bow the knee to God's truth.

What, we could ask, would move someone who is thinking this way from being satisfied with no explanation of the origin of the universe to an urge to know its origin? This question moves us to the persuasive or rhetorical value of the First Cause proof. Suppose we were discussing this proof with Bertrand Russell, or someone like him, and he explained to us that our First Cause proof required the question, "What caused God?" What might our response be to this question?[6]

An answer to this question that highlights the persuasive force of apologetics brings together all that we have said thus far in this book. We remember, as we discussed in chapter 1, that the Lord "connects" to us

---

6. For an example of a possible dialogue between an unbeliever and a Christian concerning the "First Cause," see K. Scott Oliphint, *Covenantal Apologetics: Principles and Practice in Defense of Our Faith* (Wheaton, IL: Crossway Books, 2013), chapter 3.

through language. He is the Lord of language, so much so that the Son Himself *is* the Word.

As the Word, He condescends to us and uses *words* so that we might know who He is and why He has placed us in His creation. When God creates people in His image, He speaks to them, and they to Him. God creates, sustains, and ensures the power of language to connect us to Him, and to each other.

We then saw that the Lord Himself is the Apologist who fights the battle between Himself and the evil forces that fight against Him. As we fight in the Lord's army, we suit up with His armor, as His soldiers. We defend the faith wearing gospel armor so that our lives and manner might reflect the Lord's own gentleness, grace, and truth.

But we engage the fight. We take the sword of the Spirit, which is the Word of God. We use words that *connect*, and we speak *the* Word, which is God's own truth, and by doing so we "strike" the enemy in the deepest recesses of his heart. Even so, we recognize that it is that Word, combined with the regenerating work of the Holy Spirit, that alone is able ultimately to persuade and to change human hearts. But we know that the Spirit works by and with the Word that we communicate to accomplish His sovereign purposes.

Now, what have we learned about the character of people who are made in God's image? We have learned that they actually know God. They know "his eternal power and divine nature" (Rom 1:20). They know God because God makes Himself known within and without them, through all He has made (Rom 1:18–20; 2:14–17). We have also seen that, in knowing God, they know what God requires of them. They know that their sin violates His character and is, therefore, worthy of death (Rom 1:32).

With this, we are better able to address Russell's question, "Who made God?" We would say to Russell that the very definition of God requires that He *not* be made or caused. We would say to him that when we use the *word* "God," we mean by it that He transcends everything else, and alone has existence in and of Himself. By "God," we mean one who is *a se*; He alone is absolutely and completely self-sufficient. If He were caused, He would not be God.

We might expect at this point that the question would come, "How do you know that God is self-sufficient?" This is a legitimate question and goes to the heart of a persuasive apologetic when "causality," or anything else, is the issue. Before we answer it, we remember Paul's approach at Athens.

Paul began his apologetic at Athens by proclaiming to his audience just exactly what this "Unknown God" was like. He told them that God was the Creator of all things, and that He was in need of nothing (Acts 17:24–25). He told them that this God sustains them with every breath they breathe (v. 25). He told them that God's plan was to populate the earth through Adam; he told them that those made by God ought to seek Him, since He is not far from any one of them (vv. 26–27).

As we have seen, the reason Paul could begin his address at Athens in this way was because he knew that he was telling his audience what they *already* knew. In one sense, he was simply reminding them of things they were suppressing. He was using *persuasion* by appealing to something that was deeply embedded within each of them.

He knew that what he was saying to them "connected," even if they would be reluctant to admit it. He took the truth of God's character and "connected" it to what God had been saying to them, through His works, all along. To put it in theological terms, Paul was connecting God's revelation of Himself in His Word with that "natural" revelation, given in and through creation, as it was resident within each of their hearts.

And now we can begin to see a little more clearly how we might answer the "Russellian" question. Even as Russell asks, "What made God?" he knows, in his heart, God's "eternal power and divine nature." In that sense, his question is just another example of the suppression of the truth. It is an attempt to refuse to admit what he actually knows.

So, one answer that could be given to Russell's question is that we know what God is like because, and *only* because, He reveals Himself to us. We might even want him to know that since God is eternal, infinite, absolute, and self-sufficient, there would be no way for temporal, finite, and dependent creatures such as us to know Him unless He communicated Himself to us, through His revelation.

It is possible that Russell may try to call foul if we answer this way. He may say to us that it is illegitimate to bring in a "religious" source like God's revelation for our answer since he could never believe such a thing. This is a fairly common objection of many who object to Christianity. They try to forbid the use of God's revelation in our response. There are at least a couple of ways to reply to this possible objection.

First, we could remind Russell that his demand was not, "Explain to me according to *my own* beliefs and in a way that *I* can believe how you know about God." Since there is basic disagreement between us, such a demand would be illegitimate. Instead, the question or objection is how *we* know that God is not caused; the objection is not asking us how an atheist can know God is not caused. It is asking how we know about this God.

Second, we could remind Russell that *any* discussion about the origin of the universe requires faith of some sort. Since there is no certain, scientific evidence (nor could there be, since no humans were there) for the origin of all things, *anything* we believe about such things is severely limited with respect to "scientific" facts. The best that we have are hypotheses, projections, and probabilities.

More positively, however, we can be confident (as was Paul at Athens) that our communication of the truth of God meets with the knowledge of God that Russell (and everyone else) has, as one who is made in God's image. That truth, as we have seen, will always be used by God the Holy Spirit to accomplish His sovereign purposes (Isa 55:10–11). So, when we communicate to Russell, or anyone like him, that we know what God is like because He has spoken, they will, deep down, recognize this God as we speak about Him. They *know* that He is their Creator.

The good news is that once we make it clear that for anyone to know God, He must reveal Himself, we have opened the door to explain to Russell the reality that knowing God, and *acknowledging* Him, can only be done when we throw ourselves on His mercy and trust His Son, who has given us the only means by which our suppression and sin are broken down. In other words, making clear to Russell that what we know and believe is dependent on what *God* has said gives us the proper entrée to explain to him, with gentleness and reverence, what God has done in history, and supremely in Christ.

In this way, we begin to see how the *word* "cause" connects us to the truth, the *logos*, of God Himself—as He ensures that all people know His "eternal power and divine nature"—so that we can move from the *word* to the *Word* Himself. So, we can see persuasion in action as we "remind" Russell of what he already knows (because God reveals it to him in and through all things), and we offer a defense of Christianity because we show him that only One who transcends the universe can provide a rational account of all that the universe is, in its mysterious depth and breadth. Apart from that, the best we have is a seemingly unending series of dependent causes, none of which can account for all that we see around us.

Here is the summary truth of the matter—as we have seen with Paul, it is *always* persuasive to discuss God and His character with those who are outside of Christ. We must do so with care, remembering to be gentle and reverent; we must be wise in our choice of times and places, and of words that we use to do so. But every discussion about God with unbelievers "connects" to them because God Himself is constantly revealing Himself, within and without, to every person He has made.

What we have outlined here holds true for other "standard" proofs for God's existence. Those proofs use notions like "contingency" or "design" in order to show that they each are in need of an explanation. Contingency can only be explained by that which is necessary, so again we can argue, based on what God has told us about Himself, that God alone is the only ground on which contingencies can have their proper explanation. So also for design. The design we see, in microcosm and in macrocosm in the universe, can only have a rational explanation in the One who is able to create such unfathomable, non-repeatable, and irreducible harmonies in the various aspects of His world.

In all of these, we take the *words*—the *logos*—that are used as connection points of persuasion, and we connect them to what God has said about Himself. Those words are the persuasive springboards that launch us into the possibility of showing what it means to trust and believe what God has said, and supremely to believe His Son.

LOGOS AND CHRISTIAN MATURITY

One of the things, perhaps the most important thing, that can help us understand the power of a persuasive apologetic is to think carefully and biblically about just exactly what we believe about Christ, and about Christianity. This may sound too obvious even to mention. Anyone who has come to Christ surely recognizes who He is and what He has done for us and for His people throughout history.

The book of Hebrews is a helpful guide to us in this regard. We have seen already that the author to the Hebrews is zealous to set forth the full deity and sufficiency of Jesus Christ. He begins the book by setting forth the Son as Himself both fully God—"The radiance of God's glory and the exact representation of his being" (Heb 1:3)—and also as the one who alone has accomplished His mission and who is now reigning at the Father's right hand, as our great High Priest. The message of Hebrews, in other words, is the message of Christ, now reigning as our King and High Priest, and interceding for us.

It might come as a surprise, then, when we read the author exhorting his readers and hearers to "move beyond the elementary teachings about Christ" (Heb 6:1). Why would an inspired author of Scripture, an author whose singular desire is to highlight the absolute deity and radical sufficiency of Christ, now urge his audience to "move beyond" Christ?

This paragraph helps us see why:

We have much to say about this, but it is hard to make it clear to you because you no longer try to understand. In fact, though by this time

181

you ought to be teachers, you need someone to teach you the elementary truths of God's word all over again. You need milk, not solid food!
Anyone who lives on milk, being still an infant, is not acquainted with
the teaching about righteousness. But solid food is for the mature, who
by constant use have trained themselves to distinguish good from evil.
(Heb 5:11–14)

The reason the author wants his audience to "move beyond" is
precisely because he is concerned for their holiness and sanctification
in Christ (Heb 12:14).

It is noteworthy that the author knows his original audience well
enough to recognize that "by this time you ought to be teachers." This
is noteworthy, not only because it tells us that the author was intimately
acquainted with those to whom he originally wrote, but also because his
expectation for them, and (because this is given to the church in Holy
Scripture) *for us*, is that all of us are expected to reach a point in our
Christian pilgrimage where we can be *teachers* of God's Word.

This does not mean that everyone in Christ's church is called to the
particular task of teaching (see Eph 4:11–13), but it does mean that all of
us, as Christ's sheep, are meant to move from the spiritual nursery to the
spiritual sanctuary. The process of sanctification in us means, at least,
that we must be diligent to advance from spiritual milk to spiritual meat
(see Eph 4:14–15).

The language used in Hebrews 5:14 gives us clues as to how we move
from the nursery to the sanctuary. We are able to digest solid, spiritual
food when "by constant use" we "train" ourselves to "distinguish good
from evil." There are some keys here that need to be highlighted.

The first key to spiritual maturity is, in a word, *habit*. When the
author says "constant use," what he means is that we are those who have
developed spiritual habits that mark the daily rhythm of our lives. In our
day and time, this can be increasingly difficult. Why so?

In Hebrews 2:1, just after the author extols the majesty and preemi-
nence of the Son, he issues a command:

We must pay the most careful attention, therefore, to what we have heard, so that we do not drift away.

In his effort to move his readers to maturity, the first thing that he signals as necessary for them is that they "must pay the most careful attention to what they have heard." In other words, they are to listen intently and thoughtfully. They are to focus their energies on those things that have been preached and taught to them. And, since these are "the last days" (Heb 1:2), they are to "pay *the most careful* attention" to the Scriptures.

With all the obvious benefits of technology, one of its detriments is that it can, almost unconsciously, produce habits in us that can harm our spiritual growth. When one of my children was in college, some twenty years ago, he eventually decided to take one of his "messaging" applications off his computer because people kept sending him messages and thwarting his ability to study.

Twenty years later, most of us have phones that are used for much more than calling people. They are messaging devices that keep us *constantly* "in touch" with family and friends, virtual and otherwise. They beg for our constant attention as we feel the urge almost incessantly to look and see, or to "text" or "post" so that we can always and at every minute be connected. This can tempt us to desire to be the focus of someone else's attention. By almost any measure, these phones produce minute-by-minute, hour-by-hour, day-by-day habits in us.

What we may not see is that these habits that they produce can seriously undermine our ability to *focus* properly on anything else. Because they are constantly with us, and because we constantly feel the need to connect or stay connected, it becomes difficult for some, and impossible for others, to *set our minds* on anything else for a sustained period of time. The habit of looking and posting and tweeting can eclipse any possibility for *sustained* thought and *focus* on other things.

So, another key to Christian maturity is that it requires prolonged and sustained effort. It requires us to "pay the most careful attention" to what we have heard and read. It requires us to develop *habits* of meditative thought and of consistent application. Like military soldiers, it requires us to *train ourselves* to focus and to think in order that we might be prepared for the battle that rages.

In one sense, apologetics can be described as "premeditated evangelism." It is evangelism, because its focus is on the gospel of Jesus Christ. We are defending the *Christian* faith, and in so doing we want people to hear about and submit to Christ our Lord and King.

But it is the "premeditation" part that can be challenging, perhaps even daunting. Premeditation requires that we develop a focus—a *mindset*—that is intent on "moving beyond" the ABCs of Christianity. It is a focus that meditates on the wonder of the Christian faith, in all of its multifaceted and magnificent beauty and harmony. It is a focus that, according to the author to the Hebrews, would qualify us to be teachers of others who are either outside of Christ, or who are still babes in the faith.

To "premeditate" is to go beyond the reading of Scripture, as vitally important as that is. If we want to "premeditate" on Scripture, we will take what we have read and focus on it for a length of time. We will turn it over in our minds, ask ourselves questions about it, pursue answers to those questions, either in the text or in other similar texts. We will take what we have read and establish connections between it and other things we have read previously. In other words, we will develop *habits* of sustained focus.

As we "premeditate" on what we have read in Scripture, or heard in a sermon, we will also ask ourselves how such truths help us understand what is happening in the world. We will be intent to see the world through the "spectacles of Scripture." This might reorient our thinking. We may recognize that the truly important events in the world are not always what we see in the headlines.

As we "premeditate," we are moving on to Christian maturity. We are also preparing ourselves to "give an answer" (1 Pet 3:15) to those who might ask us about our faith, or who might challenge what we believe. Premeditation is crucial for spiritual growth; it is also crucial for a persuasive apologetic.

Another key to Christian maturity is that our "paying the most careful attention," our development of spiritual habits, our dedication to training ourselves, and our premeditation, are all intended to enable us to "distinguish good from evil."

John Calvin's comments on this, as they bring together much that we have been discussing, are worth considering:

> And such he would have all Christians to be, such as have attained by continual practice a *habit* to discern between good and evil. For we cannot have been otherwise taught aright in the truth, except we are fortified by his protection against all the falsehoods and delusions of Satan; for on this account it is called the *sword of the Spirit*. And Paul points out this benefit conferred by sound doctrine when he says, "That we may not be carried about by every wind of doctrine" (Eph 4:14). And truly what sort of faith is that which doubts, being suspended between truth and falsehood? Is it not in danger of coming to nothing every moment?[7]

In other words, our pilgrimage in sanctification and holiness should move us to habitually immerse ourselves in Scripture so that, being rooted in God's own truth, we are able more and more to discern what is agreeable, and what is opposed, to that Word of truth. This is exactly what Adam and Eve should have done. Their sinful confusion over "good and evil" betrayed their lack of trust in the Word of the Lord.

MATURITY AND PERSUASION

But what does all of this focus on Christian maturity have to do with persuasion and apologetics? Surely, at any level of Christian maturity, we can commend and defend the faith that he embraces, can't we? Yes, we can.

---

7. John Calvin and John Owen, *Commentary on the Epistle of Paul the Apostle to the Hebrews* (Bellingham, WA: Logos Bible Software, 2010), 129, my emphases.

But we should also recognize that the better we know the faith to which we are committed, the better able we are to explain it. Why is that? There is a four-part answer to that question.

1. The Universality of Christianity

First, as we grow more and more into adult Christians, moving from spiritual milk to spiritual meat, from the nursery to the sanctuary, we recognize more and more that the truth of the Christian faith applies to everything, and to everyone, universally.

C. S. Lewis put it this way: "I believe in Christianity as I believe that the sun has risen: not only because I see it, but because by it I see everything else."[8] The point Lewis is making, and the first point of Christian maturity, is that our Christian faith is meant to expand beyond my own personal salvation, as important as that is. Once we grasp that Christianity is true *for me*, we are meant to "move beyond" its personal application toward its application for all of life. Yes, I believe Christianity because, as Lewis says, by God's grace "I see it." But, in pressing on to maturity, we are also recognizing that the truth of Christianity shapes and molds how we think about everything else as well.

As we move from the personal to the universal, we begin to recognize that Christianity is not only true *for me*, but that it is *true*, whether or not I believe it. In other words, growing in Christ means, in part, that we see the truths of what God has said as *universal* truths, truths that apply to all people, everywhere, and at all times.

For example, I do not simply believe that *I* am created in God's image; I believe that *all* people are created in God's image. I believe, as Paul said to the Athenians, that "*From one man* [God] made all the nations, that they should inhabit the whole earth; and he marked out their appointed times in history and the boundaries of their lands" (Acts 17:26, emphasis mine). In other words, to believe Christianity is to believe, not that we are a product of time plus chance plus matter, but that we are all descendants

---

8. C. S. Lewis, *C. S. Lewis Essay Collection and Other Short Pieces* (New York: HarperCollins, 2000), 21.

of Adam, and that we are who we are by virtue of God's own design and direction.

As John Calvin put it, we are to see everything through the spectacles of Scripture.[9] As with our physical eyeglasses, God's own truth is meant to be the "corrective lenses" through which we view the entire world. Christian maturity manifests itself in us, more and more, as we view this world and everyone and everything in it more and more from the perspective of the Christian story.

For example, what does it mean that there is "no other name" under heaven by which we can be saved (Acts 4:12)? This is one of the most offensive teachings of Christianity, according to some. It is offensive because it looks intolerant, exclusive, and narrow-minded. But, if we think about it and recognize the universality of this truth, its exclusivity is actually a product of its universal *inclusiveness*.

In other words, the truth of Christianity is not "Christianity is for me and not for you." Instead, because God now "commands all people everywhere to repent" (Acts 17:30), Christianity is applicable to *everyone, everywhere*. The reality that there is "no other name" by which we can be saved applies universally. The reason some are excluded from Christianity is not the fault of Christianity, but rather is the fault of the ones who will not repent and believe.

2. The Futility of Rebellion

Second, once we develop the habit of seeing this entire world as "my Father's world," as the old hymn puts it, we will also begin to see the utter futility of living life apart from, and in rebellion against, God and His truth. If people were truly a product of time plus chance plus matter, a cosmic "accident" that might or might not have occurred, then there is no possibility of "adding" human dignity, human significance, or human flourishing to such an existence. If we believe that we are merely

---

9. See, for example, John Calvin, *Institutes of the Christian Religion*, ed. John T. McNeill, trans. Ford Lewis Battles, vol. 1, The Library of Christian Classics (Louisville, KY: Westminster John Knox Press, 2011), 160–61.

accidental occurrences in an accidental world and we are consistent with our own beliefs, then those things that we tend to prize the most—things like love, and kindness, and truth, and significance—are all fantasies and illusions. They cannot be produced by a chance collection of matter.

It has been said that those who are experts at detecting counterfeit money develop their expertise, not by studying a multitude of counterfeit bills, but by knowing what real money looks like so well, in every detail, that a counterfeit bill would be immediately recognized. The same is true with Christianity. The more we know and meditate on the truth of Christianity in its multifaceted and universal dimensions, the more readily that which is contrary to the truth stands out in bold relief.

When we immerse ourselves in the truth of Scripture and "move beyond" the elementary aspects of it in order to see its universal application, we should be struck, again and again, with the bankruptcy of unbelieving thought and practice. Even as we recognize our own bankruptcy apart from the grace of God, we will notice, more and more, how vapid and empty life is apart from Christ.

When we notice this, we will be moved to humility and compassion. We will pray more for those we know who are in rebellion against God. We will be more aware of the emptiness and restlessness of our friends and acquaintances who do not know Christ. Knowing the Lord better, and seeing our own futility apart from Him, will cause us to long for the repentance and conversion of others whom we know and love. It will move us to a desire to attempt persuasively to communicate the good news of Christ, and to defend that good news against objections that might come against it.

3. The Foreign Aspects of Life

Third, as we "move beyond" the elementary aspects of our faith, and as we grow in the grace and knowledge of Jesus Christ more and more (2 Pet 3:18), and as we see more clearly the vanity and bankruptcy of unbelief in our friends and acquaintances, we will also begin to notice that there are things in their lives that (1) are extremely important to them, and that (2) are "foreign" to their commitment to unbelief and to rebellion against God.

The second of these needs a bit of explanation, but given what we have discussed previously, it should resonate with us fairly easily. What do we mean by things that are "foreign" to unbelief? Maybe an illustration will help. Whenever a person receives an organ transplant, one of the primary concerns is that the organ might be rejected by its new body. Why would, say, a kidney from one body be rejected by another body? The layperson's answer to that question is that the body which now has the transplanted organ detects something "foreign" in it and so the immune system rallies to try to destroy it. It is the same kidney, from the first person to the second. But in the second person, the kidney may not "fit." It can be detected as a foreign substance.

Let's suppose that someone is committed to some naturalistic view of macro-evolution as the "answer" to his origin, and the origin of human beings more generally. With this commitment, he is supposing that all of us, over a period of time, have been accidentally produced by a random genetic process. This commitment assumes that there is no real purpose in the world, there is no real significance in the world, and there is no goal for us or for anyone else. How could there be if we are an accidental collection of matter?

But people who believe such things find it impossible to live according to those beliefs. Instead, they affirm purpose, significance, meaning, and goals. In spite of their commitment to their own purely material existence, they speak freely and readily about such "non-material" things as love, kindness, joy, grief, happiness, good, and evil. In most cases, when someone with these commitments dies, there is a eulogy that affirms that there is something good, something better after death.

The question for us is this: Where did these "non-material" aspects of life come from, if macro-evolution is true? The short answer is that such things can have no place in a world where all that exists is matter plus time plus chance. As a matter of fact, there is no theory of macro-evolution, or of any other theory of origins (except Christianity), that can account for the fact that human beings are unique in creation. There is no theory of origins that can account for the fact that human beings have minds (not just brains) and so participate in an intricate and complex series of "non-material" activities in their day-to-day lives. Instead, it is just these "non-material" aspects of our lives that provide the uniqueness of who we are as human beings.

Like a transplanted organ, such things as love, joy, grief, kindness, and happiness are "foreign" elements in a non-Christian "body." And here is the biblical truth of the matter: the only way that people who are outside of Christ can participate in love and joy, etc. is because they are made in the image of God, and in knowing God, they "transplant" those things that are only meant for Christianity into the "foreign" body of their unbelieving lives. Those wonderful aspects of what it means to be human cannot easily reside within a "body" that is accidental in the universe, and that claims no uniqueness. If the unbeliever is consistent, he would need to reject all such aspects of our humanity, since his own life is a cosmic accident.

4. The Impossibility of the Contrary

This leads us to our fourth aspect of the relationship of Christian maturity to persuasive apologetics. When we recognize those "foreign" elements in the lives and thinking of those who are apart from Christ, we may begin to help them see how these elements, which they themselves are committed to and which play such significant roles in their own daily lives, are actually only really "at home" in the original "body" of Christianity.

In other words, it might help if we can lead people to see that some of the most significant aspects of their own lives are, as a matter of fact, "foreign" to their own commitments and beliefs about themselves. They are foreign organs, taken from the original body of Christianity and transplanted into the foreign body of unbelief. To the extent that they would be consistent with their own commitments to unbelief, their unbelief would reject those foreign elements and destroy them. They have no place in a world that is only material and accidental.

We could think about this plight more broadly. The persuasive aspect of this approach to a defense of Christianity can be called "the impossibility of the contrary." As we think about Christianity, and as we "move beyond" the basic aspects of it in order to grow into Christian adults, we recognize that the Bible's teaching that there is no other name by which people can be saved includes the fact that there is *no other truth* available to people than Christian truth.

It is not as though Christians have some truth and science has some truth and philosophy has some truth, and what we need is to merge all these truths together in order to have the complete truth. Instead, all truth is God's truth, so whatever truth there is in any and all disciplines, is true because of who God is and because of what He has said in His revelation to us (both in creation and in Scripture).

I remember, over four decades ago, watching the film series by the late Francis Schaeffer entitled, *How Should We Then Live?* In that series (and in the book by the same name), he gave an illustration of what we mean by "the impossibility of the contrary" in Western thought. In his description of the history of philosophy in the film series, Schaeffer said this:

> The history of this train of non-Christian philosophers could be pictured like this: One man would say, "Here is a circle which will give the unified and true knowledge of what reality is . . ." The next man would say, "No!" and cross out the circle . . . Then he would say, "Here is the circle . . ." A third would say, "No!" cross out that circle and say, "Here is the circle." And so on through the centuries. Each one showed that the previous philosophers had failed and then tried to construct his answer, which future thinkers would again show to be inadequate . . . [10]

---

10. Francis Schaeffer, *How Should We Then Live?* (Old Tappan, NJ: Fleming H. Revell, 1976), 151–52. This series, though dated, is still relevant as an example of "the impossibility of the contrary" apologetic applied through various stages of Western history.

Schaeffer's point, as he goes on to explain, is that it is just not possible to insert love or significance or meaning into a way of thinking, or of living, that begins with ourselves or with the universe *alone*. Every system of thought that has tried to do that has failed. There is no unified theory of ourselves and the universe, except in Christianity.

In this quote, Schaeffer is affirming how the history of Western thought has demonstrated that it is impossible to think or live according to any ideas or practices that are conjured up by ourselves alone. Anything, in other words, that is contrary to Christianity is completely unable to address the real circumstances of daily life and thought—this is "the impossibility of the contrary." Anything contrary to Christianity is impossible consistently to think, or to live.

The good news for a persuasive apologetic is that any and every human-centered way of thinking or living *must* borrow aspects of Christianity in order to live in God's world. The persuasive challenge is for us to identify those borrowed aspects and to try to show how neatly and properly they fit into Christianity. We might want to do this, at times, by asking questions that would highlight how "foreign" such things are apart from Christianity. This would highlight the "persuasive pinch."

We might, for example, say something like, "If you and I are simply a product of matter and time and chance, how can the love we have for our spouse be anything more than a material reaction in our material bodies?" A question like that could be fruitful (and we will remember to ask such questions in gentleness and with reverence), and could lead any number of good directions.

Or, we may want to take those things that our non-Christian friends have "borrowed," and that they affirm, and explain to them their "original" meaning and context in light of Christian truth. We may want to explain to them that the only view that makes sense of our human thinking, and acting, and reacting in the world is one that acknowledges an original One who Himself thinks and acts. The only reasonable position to hold, in other words, is that the human mind and personality come from One who is personal and who knows all things. No other view of the origin of human beings has been able to account for such significant, central, crucial human uniqueness and human activities.

Or, we may want to do both, in various ways. We show the bankruptcy of unbelieving ideas and purposes, and also show how such universal and necessary virtues like love and kindness have to have their home in Christian truth, given in God's revelation.

In any case, the persuasive aspect of this approach recognizes that we are *taking something that they already affirm* and "drawing them in," as it were, to the Christian context by showing that what they affirm has its meaning and significance in God's world and in God's truth, rather than in the context of their own beliefs.

NO OTHER NAME

In thinking of the *logos* of persuasion—the actual argument that we can offer—we could outline it this way: we take what they affirm, but what they cannot account for given their own rebellion and unbelief, and try to show how such crucial aspects of their lives cannot "fit" with what they believe and affirm about themselves, and about human beings generally. Or, we take what they affirm, but what they cannot account for, and try to show how such things have their proper home in God's world and with God's truth alone. In many cases, we might want to argue in both of these ways.

As we have seen, this is what the apostle Paul does in Athens. He quotes two Greek poets, recognizing that his audience would have known them both. He takes what they already affirm in those poets and he explains to them how such things can only be *truly* affirmed within the context of who the true God, not the "Unknown God," is and what He has done.

When we are focusing on the *logos* of a persuasive apologetic, we focus, as we have said, on the actual arguments that can be persuasive. The argument we have discussed in this section—an argument from "the impossibility of the contrary"—can be applied and set forth, no matter what the context or content of a person's unbelieving position is. That is the positive side of this argument.

The challenging aspect to this kind of argument is that it is not a "one size fits all" argument. It cannot be prepared beforehand in such a way that it will apply to every person in exactly the same way. While certain principles and processes can certainly be anticipated beforehand, it is usually best, in an argument like this, to talk with the person first, in order to see more exactly what the precise commitments are, and to ascertain what this person believes and maintains. This reminds us of the importance of *pathos* for a persuasive apologetic.

Commitments, needs, questions, and desires can vary from person to person, and can even vary within individuals, depending on circumstances. So, we can be ready to give an answer to any person at any time, with this kind of argument, but we may nevertheless need some more particular and specific information before we can address the issue in a way that "connects" more readily to them.

This is where our "premeditated evangelism" can come in handy. If we have been thinking about Scripture, and if we have been viewing the world in light of what Scripture says, we will be more ready and able persuasively to deal with questions and objections that may come to us. As we meditate on God's truth, we are "paying much more attention" to it, and we are preparing ourselves to "move beyond" the basics of Christianity, to maturity so that we might be able to teach others of this truth.

There is "no other name" under heaven by which anyone can be saved. Not only so, but Jesus Christ *alone* is the Truth. He now reigns at the right hand of His Father, while a footstool is being made for His feet. That footstool will consist of the myriad enemies that He has subdued, and will continue to subdue, throughout history. Just as He subdued us, His people, so will He continue to subdue them until He returns (1 Cor 15:25).

We are given the inestimable privilege of being construction workers with Him, as He uses us, His servants, to help build His footstool.

When we conduct ourselves with wisdom toward outsiders, making the most of every opportunity (Col 4:5), we work to persuasively defend the faith, once for all given to the saints (Jude 3). And, if the Lord should allow, the truth that we set forth, which is the sword of the Spirit, might be used by the Holy Spirit of God to open the eyes of the blind, that they too might be transferred from the kingdom of darkness to the kingdom of His marvelous light (1 Pet 2:9).

CONCLUSION

We referred to this verse earlier, but it bears repeating, and a little focus, as we conclude:

> Be wise in the way you act toward outsiders; make the most of every opportunity. Let your conversation be always full of grace, seasoned with salt, so that you may know how to answer everyone. (Col 4:5–6)

Persuasion in apologetics is always a matter of wisdom. Wisdom is the application of what we know to the particular situation confronting us. Because situations differ, the *application* of what we know will differ as well. So, we need wisdom at every step.

We can see in these two verses that there is an apologetic focus. We are to exercise wisdom, with speech full of grace and "saltiness," so that we might know how to answer everyone. As we saw in 1 Peter 3:15, we are encouraged to learn how to respond to people who ask us about our faith. As Peter puts it, we are to know how to answer everyone. Paul has the same idea in mind in these verses from Colossians.

As we think about the Christian virtue of wisdom, how ought we to view our persuasive apologetic? If we were to use the analogy of a recipe, Paul gives us four crucial ingredients, all of which are intended together to produce the tasty dish of a persuasive apologetic response.

First, we are to be *wise* in our response. As we noted above, wisdom is always "for the moment" so its specific application is difficult to set out ahead of time. We should recognize, however, that wisdom requires a proper, biblical assessment of a given situation. It requires, in other words, a recognition that not every situation will call for an identical response from us. To think all situations and concerns are identical is to lack wisdom. Wisdom requires biblical discernment.

Second, this is why Paul encourages us to *"make the most of the opportunity."* If we were to assume that our response in a previous situation is automatically adequate and relevant in a current, different situation, we may be wasting our time instead of redeeming it. If we respond, for example, to someone who rejects Christianity because of the hypocrisy within it in the exact same way that we respond to someone who rejects Christianity because it seems unscientific, we are not being wise in our response, and we are not effectively using the time available to us. Each of those two objections deserves a Christian response, but wisdom dictates that the responses might differ in significant ways.

Third, no matter the question, the objection, or the topic, we see to it that our "conversation be *full of grace.*" The word translated "conversation" here is the word we are now familiar with, *logos*. Here we are reminded that our message, even as it communicates the truth of Scripture, should always be a message of grace. In other words, our response to objections should not automatically be one of condemnation and accusation, but should be one of salvation and redemption. As subjects of God's saving grace ourselves, we should be mindful of showing that grace to those who have not experienced it. If they see no grace in us, it will be very difficult for them to see grace in God Himself.

Fourth, Paul says our conversation—our *logos*—should be "seasoned with salt." This is the only time Paul uses the word "salt" in his entire corpus of letters. Some think Paul's use here is meant to encourage us to be winsome in our conversation. Or maybe Paul uses this metaphor to remind us to make our conversation palatable to the ones to whom we speak. Whatever precisely Paul has in view, a "salty" conversation, a salty *logos*, is surely different from one that is bland and vapid.

In Paul's use of "salt" here, there can be little doubt that he means that a wise conversation that makes the most of the time we are given, and that is full of grace, is one that is meant to be "tasted" by those to whom we speak. That is, what we say in a persuasive conversation should not be full of disconnected words and ideas. We should attempt to "connect" our conversation with the concerns, questions, objections, or concepts that the other person articulates. Thus, "saltiness" is a central aspect of persuasion because it results in others "tasting" or experiencing what we say in our conversations with them.

We have already seen that, because of God's activity in revealing Himself in and through all of creation, we can "connect" our persuasive conversation to other people by communicating to them the truth of God as it is given in Scripture. When we communicate that truth, it is "tasted" by others, because they already know the God of whom we speak.

In other words, there is something deep inside all of us that is intrinsic to who we are as human beings, created in God's image. If people are not going to simply hear what we say to them, but to "taste" it, there must be an internal "connection," a connection that reaches into the inner recesses of the soul and resides there, to be "digested" according to God's own purposes. To make these connections requires wisdom—and wisdom, for most of us, takes practice.

When we think of the wisdom of persuasion, we remember that, as with the deep-seated instincts of motherhood, there is, in every person, a deep-seated knowledge of God that can never be completely erased. As we have seen, this knowledge of God is inevitably suppressed, but it remains in all of us, nevertheless.

Conducting ourselves with wisdom toward outsiders means, at least, that we try to recognize that resident, deep-seated knowledge of God in our conversations with those who are outside of Christ. Not only will we see it in its suppression, as people refuse to honor God or give Him thanks, but we will see it in its inadvertent manifestations as well, as people "borrow" from Christian truth in order to try to make sense of their own lives.

With wisdom, we earnestly try to see these aspects of people's lives in our conversations so that, full of grace and seasoned with salt, we might connect with their concerns and questions. Then, if we are able to connect, we pray that the Lord will take the truth we communicate and, by His Spirit, draw them to Himself.

I hope, by this point, the progression of persuasion in apologetics is much more obvious than it was at the beginning of this book. We began with the simple, though profound, truth that persuasion begins where everything else begins—with the Lord Himself. It begins because, and only because, at creation, the Lord decided to condescend to *speak* to and with those made in His image.

Not only did the Lord speak to His human creatures, but He walked and talked with them throughout redemptive history. The Lord could have simply spoken from heaven. He could have communicated to us without ever coming to earth to walk and talk to us. But He did much more than just speak. He condescended to be with us on the earth He had made.

Not only so, but in speaking *words* to us, He came to us *as the Word Himself*. He appeared, at various times and places, throughout the Old Testament. But He appeared, climactically and finally, as He took on a human nature in the person of the Son of God (Heb 1:1–4). Surely, there could be no other more perfect, more majestic, more incomprehensible, more meaningful example of persuasion than this. The Lord did not simply speak to us from heaven. Instead, "heaven came down," as the Word Himself, and became one of us, so that we might know the Lord, and trust in Him alone for our salvation (John 6:38).

Even as the Divine Persuader, the Lord is also the Divine Defender. Though slow to anger, He will not let the guilty go unpunished. He is the Lord of hosts, the Commander of the army, the One who leads the fight against rebellion and unbelief. He fights with the weapons of the Messianic Warrior. Those weapons are given to those who are united to

Him by faith. The weapons He uses to fight the good fight, He also gives to His people, that we might fight behind Him, our Divine Warrior.

As a matter of fact, anything we can do as persuasive apologists depends, in the first place, on the Lord Himself, who is *the* Faithful Apologist. He fights the good fight; He uses whatever means He deems fit in order to draw His people to Himself. One of those means includes His people.

As we seek to follow our Faithful Apologist, we fight the Lord's battle in the Lord's way. As we recognize our own responsibility faithfully to persuade in our defense of Christianity, we also glory in the truth that it is the Spirit alone who is able to change hard hearts. Because our Faithful Apologist is also a Faithful Persuader, we can rest in our attempts at persuasively defending the faith, recognizing that He calls us to faithfully communicate His truth. Our success is tied, not to the conversion of those to whom we speak, but to our faithfulness in expressing what He has told us.

It should be clearer now that we've reached the end of our study that persuasive apologetics is something every Christian can engage in. It does not depend on our academic status; it does not depend on our ability to construct logical proofs for God's existence; it certainly does not require us to develop a "sales program" in order to peddle the gospel.

Instead, a persuasive apologetic is accomplished when we have a proper, biblical focus on (1) our own Christian character (*ethos*), (2) the person(s) to whom we are speaking, and (3) the gospel message that we desire to communicate. With those things in view, the Spirit of God will use the truth of God in His own sovereign way, and He uses that truth, at times, to bring His own people to Himself. Since the Lord has asked us to make ourselves ready to defend the Christian faith (1 Pet 3:15), we can be confident that He will give us what we need to accomplish that task. The Faithful Apologist is always faithful to provide what His children need.

In summing up our entire discussion about persuasive apologetics, it hinges on three magnificent and majestic words—"God has spoken." He spoke to Adam and Eve in the garden. He created language—words—that

He might interact with them, and they with Him. He has spoken in and through all He has made.

Because He continues to speak within and outside of us, we all know Him. He has spoken in His Son, the Word, who became one of us in order to persuade His people, to draw them to Himself.

Now, in "these last days" (Heb 1:2), He continues to speak by His Word—the Holy Scriptures—and by His Spirit. Any and all persuasion is fulfilled when the Word and the Spirit change human hearts of stone to hearts of flesh. And the Lord has graciously given us, His people, the privilege of engaging in the wisdom of a persuasive apologetic, so that His footstool might continue to be built, as His enemies are subdued and become, by His grace, His friends, even His own dear children.